T0209148

Gen-eXceptional

Gen-eXceptional

*How the Unique Traits of Generation X
Can Transform Leadership*

Robert F. DeFinis, EdD

 iUniverse®

GEN-EXCEPTIONAL
HOW THE UNIQUE TRAITS OF GENERATION X
CAN TRANSFORM LEADERSHIP

iUniverse books may be ordered through booksellers or by contacting:

iUniverse
1663 Liberty Drive
Bloomington, IN 47403
www.iuniverse.com
844-349-9409

Because of the dynamic nature of the Internet, any web addresses or links contained in this book may have changed since publication and may no longer be valid. The views expressed in this work are solely those of the author and do not necessarily reflect the views of the publisher, and the publisher hereby disclaims any responsibility for them.

Any people depicted in stock imagery provided by Getty Images are models, and such images are being used for illustrative purposes only.
Certain stock imagery © Getty Images.

ISBN: 978-1-6632-5760-4 (sc)
ISBN: 978-1-6632-5762-8 (hc)
ISBN: 978-1-6632-5761-1 (e)

Library of Congress Control Number: 2023921513

Print information available on the last page.

iUniverse rev. date: 11/08/2023

Contents

Part III: Shaping the Future of Leadership

Interface

"Gen-eXceptional: How the Unique Traits of Generation X Can Transform Leadership," is a transformative guide that delves into the exceptional leadership qualities of Generation X and their distinct ability to navigate the complexities of contemporary leadership in a rapidly evolving world.

Part I of the book uncovers the essence of Gen X, exploring the foundational experiences and values that shape their innovative approach to leadership. This section probes the defining characteristics that set Gen X apart, revealing how they stand out within the broader spectrum of generations in the modern workforce.

Part II illuminates the dynamic leadership styles inherent to Gen X, which seamlessly blend traditional wisdom with cutting-edge strategies for the digital age. Unveiling the core principles of Gen X leadership, this section highlights their commitment to authenticity and their ability to draw from a wealth of experience to lead with unwavering conviction. Furthermore, it explores their unique skill in striking a harmonious balance between technological advancements and meaningful human connections.

Part III propels us into the future of leadership, showcasing how Gen Xers are at the forefront of driving transformative change. By assuming the role of change catalysts, they bring their adaptable nature to the fore, paving the way for new directions and innovations. Through mentorship and by nurturing emerging talent, Gen X leaders ensure a sustainable legacy of leadership excellence across generations. This section culminates in a profound exploration of the evolving landscape of Gen X leadership, projecting their enduring influence and contributions.

"Gen-eXceptional" encapsulates the remarkable journey of Generation X, offering invaluable insights into their distinct leadership strengths and how these strengths are poised to shape the trajectory of leadership in the 21st century. This book is an indispensable resource for leaders of all ages and backgrounds, providing actionable wisdom and strategies that transcend generational boundaries.

PART I

Unveiling Generation X

1

Introduction to Generation X

Generation X (i.e., Gen X) members, commonly known as Gen Xers, were born between 1960s and early 1980s. While they have often been overshadowed by their predecessors, the Baby Boomer generation, and their successors, the aging Millennials, Gen Xers have significantly contributed to popular culture analysis, which is worth further exploring. Gen Xers have had an indisputable effect on societal trends worldwide that should be duly acknowledged, from fashion to technology to music.

Understanding Gen X: Who They Are

Gen X, often overlooked compared to Baby Boomers and Millennials, is sometimes referred to as the "forgotten middle" of generations due to its lack of representation in popular culture. Nevertheless, this cluster has notably influenced American society and civilization over recent decades. Gen Xers constitute an assorted batch composed of people who were brought up in two-parent households and those from single-parent homes.

The values and perspectives of Gen Xers were profoundly influenced by their parents' experiences with war, civil rights movements, feminism, and economic hardship, resulting in them being independent thinkers who cherish diversity in thought but, at the same time, regard family life highly. In contrast to Baby Boomers, who accepted traditional beliefs such as matrimony and loyalty over a prolonged period to one employer, Gen Xers have been known for adopting a more lenient attitude toward such matters; they advocate that acquiring multiple jobs or having different partners is not only acceptable, but considerably facilitates personal growth prospects. At their age, Gen Xers do not just focus on increasing financial gain like most Boomers did; instead, they prioritize achieving a work-life balance.

Gen Xers are often stereotyped as being pessimistic or indifferent regarding politics, mostly due to having grown up during an epoch marked by the Watergate scandal and Vietnam War draft dodges, when in reality they tend to possess strong views on numerous issues impacting society today, such as healthcare reform or immigration policy. Gen Xers, however, tend to not speak out due to their laid-back personalities and lack of political representation, given that political parties currently in power are mainly run by older generations like Boomers and emerging Millennials. Given that Gen X is a fundamental component of American society whose impact will continue increasing, comprehending what makes Gen Xers unique is vital to incorporating them into the current social climate.

Gen X vs. Aging Millennials: A Comparative Study

Gen X is frequently referred to as the "forgotten generation" as it stands between Baby Boomers and Millennials. Born between approximately 1965 and 1980, Gen Xers have experienced considerable economic, social, and technological alterations during their lifetimes. As Gen Xers witnessed how technology completely transformed how people relate with one another socially and labor-wise, amuse themselves recreationally, and attain knowledge about their environment, they possess diverse beliefs, values, and lifestyles.

Gen Xers tend to highly esteem their autonomy, more than all generations before them. As a result of this inclination toward individualism, Gen Xers are more prone to being skeptical of powerholders or traditional organizations like government and religion in comparison with both baby boomers and millennials. Also, Gen Xers tend to have less trust in big businesses currently than they did in the industrial age, with numerous of them regarding corporate structures as overly repressive instead of profiting society overall.

Besides having an autonomous attitude toward life, Gen Xers are pioneers in embracing digital technology inside their private lives and in the professional domain. Gen X laid the groundwork for today's digital economy by introducing new technologies such as home computers, cell phones, and online banking systems into everyday life. Thanks to these developments, Gen Xers tend to be tech-savvy adults who can navigate complex digital landscapes seamlessly—something even Millennials may find troublesome.

This unique blend of independence with technical know-how has enabled them to be incredibly successful entrepreneurs over recent decades, founding some of the most innovative existing companies, like Google, Amazon, and Uber, and contributing to environmental causes via MoveOn.org. It is thus apparent that Gen X continues to make its mark on society despite being often overlooked amidst discussions regarding Millennials taking further control.

The Impact of Baby Boomers on Gen X

The demographic cohort that follows the Baby Boomers, commonly called Gen Xers, are often described as independent, resourceful, and adaptable individuals; they have also been noted for their skepticism toward authority and willingness to query traditional values and institutions. The preceding Baby Boomer generation has had an immense effect on Gen X due to its impact on culture, technology, and economics, which form part of what shaped them into adulthood.

Regarding technology, Gen Xers were confronted with the surge of computers in daily life throughout their developmental years. It enabled them to create tech-savvy competencies that are indispensable for succeeding within the modern economy. Concerning economics, Baby Boomers had a noteworthy effect on Gen X due to their usage practices during the 1970s and 1980s that increased inflation levels across the globe.

The repercussions that Baby Boomers have had on Gen Xers can be transcribed in the social values and political beliefs of Gen X. These repercussions resulted in many younger individuals feeling uncertain about their financial future, generating a heightened level of financial insecurity among Gen Xers compared to previous generations (e.g., baby boomers who experienced economic stability for much of their lives).

As Gen Xers began transitioning into adulthood, civil rights movements were becoming increasingly influential worldwide, leading to them developing more progressive views than prior generations, such as Baby Boomers. These new-found perspectives drove many Gen Xers to start engaging in activism for causes like gender equality, LGBTQ rights, environmental protection, and beyond.

It can be concluded that while Gen X was impacted profoundly by both the Silent Generation and the Greatest Generation, Gen X's distinguishing characteristics were chiefly determined by the preceding Baby Boom generation. Although these two cohorts may have experienced divergent life situations due to historically significant events occurring at contrasting points within each epoch, there is no denying their respective contributions toward molding our current understanding of modern generations today.

Analyzing Societal Trends in the Era of Gen X

Gen X is the first generation that grew up with computers in their residences and the last one before widespread internet usage became prevalent. Consequently, they have gone through numerous societal trends exclusive to their age group.

A noteworthy shift that has taken place over Gen Xers' lifetimes is the growth in technology and its incorporation into our day-by-day lives. Technological advances have profoundly affected how people interact and access information and how businesses operate, providing new opportunities for those who are prepared to accept and use them. Moreover, globalization has caused a rise in competition within many industries and facilitated cross-cultural exchanges between nations worldwide.

Gen Xers were some of the first to experience these alterations directly; they observed items becoming more easily accessible due to global trade arrangements and started communicating with people on the other side of the earth through email or text message as opposed to relying upon traditional means like post-delivery or telephone conversations.

Gen Xers have also witnessed considerable changes in attitudes toward gender roles in society. While women still experience inequalities in some domains today, there is no denying that advancement has been made since this generation came of age to accomplish greater equality for both genders regarding education, job prospects, and wages earned.

Moreover, during the lifetime of Gen Xers, there was greater acceptance for members of various sexual orientations than in preceding eras; this includes Marriage Equality becoming legally recognized throughout much of North America by 2015, after many years of endeavors from LGBTQ activists who were pushing for equal rights under the law for all couples, regardless of their gender identity or sexual orientation.

In addition, Gen Xers have indeed played a role in fostering the trend toward environmentalism that has been spreading over the recent decades across most parts of North America through initiatives, such as recycling programs, campaigns promoting energy conservation, and consumer boycotts against organizations that engage in unethical practices, etc. Nevertheless, much more is to be done to protect our planet effectively from harmful climate change effects and other damage caused by human activities today.

Cultural and Historical Context

Gen X, born between 1965 and 1980, has been neglected in terms of media coverage and popular culture, primarily eclipsed by the Baby Boomers who preceded them as well as the Millennials who followed. Nonetheless, Gen X stands out for having grown up amidst significant changes with regards to economic and technological progressions, with personal computers (PCs) entering homes, plus an increase in awareness on a global scale. Due to these factors, Gen X is generally characterized as being more skeptical than prior generations yet also autonomous-inclined and attuned to self-reliance. Considering Gen X from a cultural and historical perspective, it is imperative to contemplate how their values were shaped by the events surrounding them during their formative years. During much of Gen Xers' childhoods, the Cold War was in progress, which unquestionably affected their viewpoint regarding life—they witnessed first-hand how abruptly situations could alter, giving them a feeling of vulnerability, but also making them aware of the importance of being equipped for any occurrence.

The arrival of technology during this era was a watershed moment for Gen Xers, who were some of the pioneers in using PCs at school and work, and even home computers such as Apple IIs, which gave people the possibility to play games or independently investigate programming languages. These technological advancements liberalized countless opportunities for ingenuity within Gen Xers, directing numerous associates from this generation toward becoming innovators in realms like Science, Technology, Engineering, Art & Mathematics.

Gen X also experienced substantial alterations in music during their formative years, with punk rock making its way out of underground scenes across North America into mainstream pop culture. Green Day is an example of a band that received considerable attention throughout the 1990s—when alternative music began to spread worldwide, dealt primarily by MTV's spreading influence. Boundaries were pushed while keeping true to tradition—something that Gen Xers are well-known for—leading many Gen Xers to adore hip-hop culture and esteem classic rock n' roll sounds from preceding decades all at once. Finally, dramatic social improvement was witnessed through movements such as LGBTQ+ rights activism, which saw unprecedented levels of acceptance over time—something nearly every Gen Xer was exposed to directly or indirectly through media coverage at some point in their life. It has undoubtedly formed perceptions on several issues connected to rights and racial injustice due to generational inclination toward increased compassion caused precisely by those same movements.

Leadership Styles of Gen X

Much debate and discussion has been devoted to the introduction of Gen X, particularly about their leadership styles. Gen X, comprised of those born between 1965 and 1980, is commonly regarded as a bridge between Baby Boomers and Millennials. Gen Xers are identified by their autonomy, skepticism toward authority figures, self-reliance, and a preference for hard work over status symbols or connections, which creates a contrast between their leadership techniques and those utilized by Baby Boomers and Millennials.

Gen X is more pragmatic in decision-making processes than Baby Boomers and Millennials, concentrating on results instead of process or procedure. This may be partially due to their upbringing in a time of rapid social transformation, which was only sometimes comprehended by earlier generations. Conversely, the likelihood of Gen X taking risks while seeking objectives or targets is lower compared to either Baby Boomer or Millennial demographics; instead, they prioritize discovering solutions that will reduce disruption while still attaining preferred outcomes.

Gen Xers prefer an open style that allows them to cooperate with their teams while maintaining autonomy and creativity; they will not micromanage; instead, they strive toward consensus among all stakeholders before making any decision regarding projects or initiatives. However, they will not hesitate to make a decision if one is needed, and consensus cannot be reached. They value transparency but seldom communicate in the same manner favored by younger generations; instead, they opt to engage in meaningful dialogue to reach an agreement on issues of varying sizes. Furthermore, Gen Xers are usually tolerant of new ideas when presented appropriately; however, if there needs to be more evidence concerning why something should prove successful versus unsuccessful, this could lead to challenges for them.

How Technology Shaped and Impacted Gen X

Dubbed the "middle child" that resides between Baby Boomers and Millennials, Gen Xers have been profoundly affected by various experiences that can be observed in their current lives. Undeniably, one of the most powerful influences for Gen X was technology. In the early years, technology significantly impacted Gen Xers, who were raised in households with computers, televisions, VCRs, video games, and other devices that enabled them to investigate novel concepts and encounters that had not been available previously. This contributed to their outlook on life by granting them access to data that was not accessible before.

Gen Xers encountered a plethora of alterations regarding communication as well, as the invention of cell phones enabled them to stay connected regardless of their location, leading to stronger relationships between individuals from different parts of the world. Furthermore, the introduction of social media platforms, such as Facebook, Instagram, and Twitter (X), enabled Gen Xers to remain informed about events occurring in their immediate circles without the need for physical meetings or even verbal exchanges via telephone calls or emails, facilitating tighter connections between friends who otherwise might have felt isolated from one another because of geographical distance or absence of time together face-to-face.

Technology has been instrumental in helping Gen Xers become more independent, as it provided them access to information right at their fingertips instead of relying solely on books or teachers for knowledge acquisition like previous generations did. Unlike preceding generations who relied on intuition because of the lack of accessibility to trusted sources, Gen Xers were able to make decisions based upon facts thanks to internet use becoming increasingly common during that period. Technological advancements have also made it much easier for them to seek employment online, giving them more flexibility when selecting career paths compared to past generations with limited routes depending largely on location.

Overall, Gen X felt a significant effect from technological advances both favorably (causing an increase in independence) and detrimentally (resulting in increased distractions). It is interesting to observe how continuous improvements continue molding future age groups while offering insight into how our lives are influenced by these shifting dynamics today.

Unraveling the Financial Habits and Choices of Gen X

Gen X possesses a position of great importance when it comes to the execution of financial planning. Being the primary iteration brought up with digital technology at their disposal, they have had experience in dealing with fluctuating economic conditions throughout their lives. As Gen Xers presently occupy ages 40 to 50, decisions regarding finances will subsequently impact their lives during retirement.

Gen Xers demonstrate distinctive financial habits and preferences regarding money management. They generally favor conservative investments compared to prior generations, partly due to their direct exposure to the stock market crash in 1987 and two recessions from 2001 through 2009. Consequently, Gen Xers are more likely to choose secure options such as mutual funds or bonds rather than taking a risk on stocks or other risky ventures.

Gen Xers are also inclined to prioritize paying off their debt rather than investing in retirement plans at the beginning; this procedure provides them with time to invest afterwards while still guaranteeing that any obligations that they have taken on will be settled earlier instead of later. The "pay yourself first" approach has become increasingly well-known among Gen Xers, who desire more control over their finances without taking too many risks at once.

Consequently, Gen X is inclined to a thriftier lifestyle than preceding generations. Older Americans can recollect existing beyond their funds during prospering periods, expecting that money matters would stay prosperous always, while Gen Xers are more inclined to save now for potential needs and difficulties in the future. Gen Xers tend to allocate 10-15% of each paycheck into savings accounts every month regardless of what they earn; should something unforeseen take place, such as job loss or medical bills, these resources could be accessed without having obtained against forthcoming revenues if there is an abrupt emergency before enough could be accumulated once again from routine payments alone.

Effects of Global Events on the Perspectives of Gen X

Global events have influenced Gen X more profoundly than any other generation. Having been the first generation to grow up in a truly internationalized world, this cohort of Americans had their formative years made memorable with numerous significant worldwide happenings such as the collapse of the Berlin Wall, the termination of apartheid in South Africa, and the dissolving of the Soviet Union. As such, these experiences have indelibly impacted how Gen Xers perceive politics, economics, social issues, and even personal identity within an international context.

Growing up during these times gave Gen Xers access to more information than was available to their predecessors which helped them understand different perspectives on global affairs and obtain insight into how other countries function politically and economically. Consequently, Gen Xers appreciate various cultures and views, as observed by their political stances—inclinations toward candidates who take a moderate stance when confronted with complex issues such as immigration or trade agreements between foreign nations.

Furthermore, Gen Xers have direct experience in perceiving how speedily technology can alter lives for better or worse—from PCs becoming run-of-the-mill in family homes around America to having the capacity to connect with individuals from all over the world through cellular phones or emails instantly. Unsurprisingly, a lot of Gen Xers are tech experts who are taking full advantage of novel possibilities generated by digital advancements, such as artificial intelligence (AI), machine learning, and big data analytics, and who recognize how quickly technology can modify our lives for good and ill.

Lastly, since Gen X was born during a period where there were still many traditional gender roles apparent in society—which included women generally staying home while men went out into public spaces—numerous Gen Xers have endeavored indefatigably across the course of their lifetimes to fashion an environment wherein everyone feels accepted regardless of their sexual orientation or gender identity. It has brought about Gen Xers being exposed advocates for diversity both inside and outside the workplace, standing up against gender stereotypes and fostering marginalized communities to enter domains traditionally governed by males, like engineering or finance industries.

2

Defining Gen X Characteristics

Gen X is an age group that has recurrently been neglected compared to the Baby Boomers and Millennials. Yet, Gen Xers have distinctive characteristics that define them and inform their lifestyle choices, such as their life objectives, career preferences, social movements. This chapter explores what it means to be a Gen Xer while examining the defining qualities of this generation.

Essential Traits and Values of Gen X

Gen X, commonly referred to as the "latchkey" generation due to their being born between 1965 and 1980 and thereby becoming the first wave of children left alone in their homes while both parents were working, is characterized by several traits that distinguish them from other generations. In terms of work-life balance, Gen Xers demonstrate an inclination toward flexibility; many members value their careers but also sustain an ardent dedication to supporting family life and personal pursuits.

Gen Xers are well known for their willingness to dedicate time and effort to completing tasks while at the same time appreciating that it is also necessary to take breaks from work to experience life outside of professional obligations. Gen X can be distinguished by its sense of autonomy; when presented with a problem or challenge, Gen Xers strive toward reaching solutions independently rather than relying on external factors for guidance.

A further characteristic of Gen X is their ability to adapt when confronted with alteration or doubt—a skill that has become even more imperative since the inception of the COVID-19 pandemic. For instance, many have been able to adjust quickly to working remotely or transitioning vocation paths within a brief span due to their high aptitude for adaptation, which makes them ideally suited for job markets subject to rapid changes such as those brought about through technological improvements over time.

In terms of values, Gen Xers tend to prioritize practicality over extravagance—which was likely fostered during this period when dual incomes were necessary to make ends meet each month. As a result, many Gen Xers focus on investing their money cautiously rather than wasting it, like some younger generations might do today. Moreover, Gen Xers are inclined to prioritize health and wellness by taking preventative measures early instead of waiting until something goes wrong before acting. This holistic approach toward health is a possible explanation as to how many Gen Xers tend to be relatively healthy throughout adulthood relative to the older generations living today.

Upbringing and Parenting Styles

Gen X possesses some other distinctive traits that set them apart. One of these attributes has to do with how their parents raised them. Gen Xers are often called "latchkey kids" as their guardians had long working hours, which forced them to be alone after school without supervision. Consequently, Gen Xers had to become highly independent at a young age and develop an intense sense of self-reliance.

Gen Xers tend to demonstrate a strong sense of self-reliance and find it effortless to make decisions independently without resorting to external advice or support. Gen Xer's parents' parenting style had an indelible impact on their mentality toward life. Their progenitors tend to possess less stringent attitudes concerning enforcement than earlier generations, thus affording Gen Xers ample latitude in trying out diverse activities and hobbies without being criticized by adults.

Gen Xers experienced a lack of structure in their upbringing, allowing them to become creative problem solvers who valued innovation over tradition when faced with new challenges or obstacles. Moreover, they had unprecedented access to technology such as computers, video game consoles, and television compared with previous generations, which enabled greater exposure to global issues and a greater comprehension of different cultures from earlier on in life than ever witnessed throughout history. Technological access also furnished direct experiences into contemporary issues, forming Gen Xers' future understanding of politics and societal dilemmas.

Growing up during an era when traditional customs like family dedication were still pervasive and yet progressive philosophies such as personal authority were becoming more prevalent, Gen Xers established a unique balance between being part of a team while remaining real individualists; they developed the abilities to accept change while respecting tradition, maintain morality while staying open-minded, take risks while concurrently maintaining reserve, and possess both autonomy yet reliability.

Shaping Historical Events

Gen X has been molded by traditional values and modern influences defining their culture and individualities. Gen Xers tend to possess independent-mindedness, self-reliance, and increased tech literacy compared to other generations; they tend to embrace varied opinions regarding life issues while valuing diversity within the work environment.

Gen Xers were brought up during the rapid advancement of technology, which has heavily impacted their outlook on life. This cohort had access to the internet from an early age and became aware firsthand of how technologies can be employed to link people worldwide—something many younger generations now take for granted. Consequently, Gen Xers maintain traditional values, such as hard work, while remaining open-minded to fresh concepts like globalization.

In addition to their technological proficiency, Gen Xers have been drastically influenced by major historical affairs such as the Cold War and the Watergate scandal, which taught them valuable lessons regarding government liability and personal accountability. Having developed amid these chaotic times has caused them to have a disposition for pragmatism; they focus less on perfect goals or indeterminate thoughts and depend more earnestly on down-to-earth strategies for tackling issues.

The social transitions initiated by Gen X have had far-reaching implications; not only did it help bring about an era of improved tolerance for diversity within society, but it also created foundations that upcoming generations would be able to take advantage of through technology— something which Millennials could never attain without Gen Xer's pioneering efforts.

Work and Career

Gen Xers' diversity can be seen in their career aspirations and job fulfillment. Gen X is highly motivated to perform well professionally and tend to seek meaningful opportunities that permit them to demonstrate their capabilities advantageously. Gen Xers also tend to be more willing than others to take risks related to professional development, potentially through business ownership or transitioning between industries or employers.

Gen Xers generally aspire for a balanced life where career development is combined with strong personal relationships—an aspiration which may sometimes elude other generations who prioritize one aspect without considering both sides equally throughout life's journey. As such, Gen Xers tend to value workplace flexibility, as it allows them greater control over the time that they spend between work responsibilities and other commitments such as family obligations or leisure activities. Workplace flexibility, which can be provided in many forms (e.g., remote working options, compressed work weeks, job-sharing arrangements), give Gen Xers an enhanced sense of freedom while ensuring that these other elements do not compromise their productivity at work.

Over the past few decades, the focus on work and career has been partially attributed to economic circumstances notably impacted by the advent of technology, globalization, and automation. Subsequently, Gen Xers have had to adopt new ways of working and rapidly adjust to endure and be successful. However, for Gen Xers to remain competitive in their respective professions, they must acquire novel abilities such as coding or data analysis, which can aid them in staying one step ahead concerning changes happening within their industry or field.

Relationships and Community

Gen X, commonly referred to as the "lost generation" due to the difficult transition between Baby Boomers and Millennials, include highly diverse members in terms of where they were born and what backgrounds they come from. Despite such differences, however, one thing that unites Gen Xers is their unique perspective on relationships and community. Gen Xers are more likely to engage in communal activities instead of individual pursuits and prefer to socialize within groups rather than alone or even in pairs.

At their core, Gen Xers emphasize establishing meaningful connections with others, including familial relations and friendships, and demonstrate comfortability when it comes to expressing themselves vocally while also respecting others' privacy. Gen Xers tend to prioritize quality relationships over quantity; they prefer having only a few close friends rather than numerous acquaintances who they do not know enough to be considered part of their inner circle.

Gen Xers are often recognized for their commitment to the communities that they inhabit, from lending aid at local events to promoting causes that hold significance to them or joining organizations designed around similar interests. Gen Xers like to participate in what is happening around them in various ways—even when it means occasionally going against societal standards.

Overall, Gen Xers strive toward creating vital online and offline connections with those near them—whether through popular social media platforms or substantive conversations held within public spaces (e.g., cafeterias, parks) which helps them to cultivate a sense of community among bigger crowds. Gen Xers take pride in comprehending their morals while recognizing how these prejudices fit into society, as this highlights their potential to not only have some influence but also to be swayed by the people surrounding them.

Technological Transformation

Gen X has encountered some of the most noteworthy technological changes that humanity has ever known. The development from PCs to internet access to smartphones is a transformation that Gen Xers witnessed firsthand; they were one of the first generations who incorporated these novel technologies into their everyday lives, earning them the moniker "digital natives." Utilizing technology, Gen X stands out for its capacity for adaptability. Gen Xers moved quickly to embrace novel technologies such as cell phones and computers, allowing them to remain connected with family members and friends in diverse parts of the world. Gen X was also adept at learning about new software applications or solving computer problems independently without relying upon external assistance from businesses or organizations that they worked for.

Additionally, there was a significant shift among this group regarding how people use technology recreationally. Video games became increasingly popular among Gen Xers who enjoyed playing them during downtime or competing against other players online as a hobby. Furthermore, Gen Xers formed part of an early cadre that adopted streaming services like Netflix, which enabled access to numerous films immediately within one's home environment instead of going out into theaters or searching through physical media stores for movies suitable enough to watch at home.

Midlife and Beyond

Possessing an unparalleled technological insight compared to earlier generations, Gen Xers are sometimes perceived as having an embedded cynicism; nevertheless, their traits extend far beyond this solitary attribute. Gen Xers have the ability to consider different perspectives before making decisions or engaging in activities; such qualities can be beneficial when contemplating significant life changes like relocating cities or launching new business ventures.

For Gen Xers, midlife can be a fascinating interval where they are still relatively youthful yet beginning to experience things like retirement planning and other mature duties while simultaneously feeling energetic enough to relish life. It is a period for Gen Xers when they can pause and contemplate their successes thus far, musing on what else must be done to reach the objectives set out for them and realize any ambitions they may possess. Numerous Gen Xers will find themselves reconciling professional objectives with family commitments and being confronted by choices regarding how they desire their lives to appear five or ten years from now; they might wonder if all their desires have already been satisfied or if something still needs to be improved concerning finance, occupation, social standing, etc.

Gen X has distinguished itself by incorporating traditional values with modern technology to contribute significantly to our present-day world's shape. As Gen X enters midlife and beyond, it is important to remember all that Gen Xers have done so far—including laying down paths for the generations that will come after them—in order to learn from their experience while at the same time keeping forward momentum toward future objectives.

3

Differentiating Gen X from Other Generations

As the world progresses and evolves, leading to further demographic shifts, comprehending how different generations vary is essential. This thought process holds especially true when discussing Gen Xers, who are often misrepresented or marginalized compared to other age cohorts. Investigating generational disparities between Gen X and alternate demographics and exploring potential methods for effectively managing intergenerational conflict amid a continuously transforming climate is vital. By looking into these topics from various perspectives, one can gain greater insight into the exclusive chances and struggles accompanying shifting demographics.

Characteristics of Baby Boomers

Baby Boomers are individuals born between 1946 and 1964, currently aged between 56 and 74. This cohort is widely known for its hardworking attitude, commitment to family values, and loyalty. Baby Boomers have worked to reach success in life and often emphasize material attainment as the primary benchmark for achievement. Additionally, Baby Boomers have been inclined toward maintaining jobs or careers over extended periods rather than taking risks when looking ahead to their economic futures.

Baby Boomers are renowned for their loyalty to, and closeness with, their families. They often assume responsibility for elderly parents or offer financial support to younger generations in need. Thus, they are dubbed "the sandwich generation" for being simultaneously required on both sides of the generational spectrum. A by-product of this vital sense of commitment is that respect is held in high esteem; not only do they expect it from others, but they also give it freely in return.

When it comes to technology, Baby Boomers have held divergent opinions over the years. Though seniors of this cohort may not be as informed about tech tools as younger generations, there has been an overall increase in Baby Boomers' utilization of these technologies due to their convenience and helpfulness within daily life routines. Baby Boomers are neither early adopters nor late in adoption rates; instead, they fall between the two extremes. Furthermore, despite being labeled by some as "old-fashioned," Baby Boomers understand that transformation is essential and can capitalize on fresh openings that result from such changes— for instance, shopping online or employing social media websites like Facebook or Instagram for professional uses.

Characteristics of Millennials

Millennials, born between 1981 and 1996, are noted for being notably diverse in their racial demographics. Knowing how to utilize technology has become second nature to Millennials as they have grown up learning about new advances within this area. The ever-evolving universe in which Millennials live has pushed them to adapt quickly and effectively to global trends and fluctuating technological developments. As such, Millennials tend to be well-educated with a heightened sense of social awareness and often demonstrate more entrepreneurial skills than prior generations, mainly due to internet access. In contrast with previous generations who typically placed importance on material items associated with status symbols, Millennials prioritize experiences, which explains why travel, food experiences, concerts, festivals, etc., are so popular among this demographic as opposed to tangible assets.

Millennials seek to augment their lives with experiences that bring them fulfillment, often searching for gainful employment, leaving sufficient time available to volunteer or join clubs and organizations. With an eye toward wellness, Millennials have developed greater mindfulness of health, evidenced by consuming organic foods, and performing regular exercise. Additionally, they have become influential participants in domestic and overseas political processes as observed by the habitually higher turnout levels at recent elections than those previously registered from other age demographics.

It is essential not to confuse the traits of Millennials with those of Gen Xers, as these two generations differ in many aspects; some examples include:

1. Their attitude toward technology use—Gen Xers may not be as tech-savvy as Millennials.

2. Gen Xers prefer stability and constancy over flexibility regarding work and life balance, while Millennials are more inclined toward taking risks.

3. Distinct parenting styles have also been observed, where Gen X parents generally emphasize traditional values such as self-discipline, while Millennial parents place a higher emphasis on emotional intelligence.

Even though there can still be parallels between these two cohorts concerning specific concerns like educational levels and environmental consciousness, one must remember to differentiate between generationally distinctive characteristics before making any inferences about an individual or group solely based on age criteria.

Characteristics of Generation Z

Generation Z (i.e., Gen Z) encompasses individuals born between 1996 and 2010. This generation has been characterized as being comprised of true digital natives due to them not having any recollection of life before the introduction of technological wonders such as smartphones, tablets, and computers; in fact, it could be argued that they have become accustomed to these devices since birth. Owing mainly in part to this early exposure, they are considered tech-savvy with an impressive ability to adapt their consumption habits accordingly.

Members of Generation Z, colloquially known as Zoomers, are considered more conscious consumers than previous generations; they consider environmental factors when making buying decisions and are interested in organizations emphasizing social responsibility.

Moreover, Gen Z is believed to differ from other generations in the following ways:

- They have higher levels of mental health understanding than all prior generations, seeing physical well-being beginning from one's psychological wellness.
- In their approach toward education, they tend to display superior multitasking abilities relative to earlier generations and prefer courses that provide practical applications rather than focusing solely on theoretical learning.
- They tend to prefer shorter educational programs to the traditional four-year college degrees because of the rising tuition fees and the growing availability of online courses and apprenticeships that offer them greater flexibility when developing new expertise or advancing their career objectives.
- They possess an independent mindset while being highly collaborative—compared to preceding generations who usually leaned toward either end—making them especially suitable for functioning within teams where collaboration is essential for success.
- They are broad-minded about dissimilar cultures, making them particularly right for international business transactions in a progressively globalized world.

Distinct Traits of Gen X in the Workforce

Gen X has been acclaimed for their independence and resourcefulness, primarily due to being raised predominantly by two working parents, forcing them to develop a self-reliant attitude and an elevated level of motivation. Gen X also exhibits keen skepticism toward authoritative figures and strongly values individualism. Gen Xers have established themselves as adept users of technology in comparison with any other age group while demonstrating an inclination toward hard work over competition or rivalry within teams-based workplace surroundings.

Given their upbringing in two-income households where they had to take on multiple roles, such as parent, childcare provider, and breadwinner, Gen Xers are very adept at multitasking. This aptitude makes them highly valuable in today's modern workplace, often beset by distractions like emails, texts, and social media notifications that can quickly compromise productivity. Furthermore, Gen Xers tend to prefer directness over ambiguity or subtlety to achieve tasks efficiently and effectively in the working environment. They also tend to possess considerable problem-solving capabilities, which give them an edge when dealing with complex projects or demanding customers or co-workers who may not share their preference for straightforward dialogue styles or efficient problem-solving approaches.

Comparison of Gen X with Other Generations in the Workforce

While Gen X may not be subjected to as much scrutiny as its predecessors or successors, it should still be acknowledged as a noteworthy force within the workforce. Gen Xers have had to form a connection that bridges Baby Boomers raised in more traditional work settings with Millennials famed for exhibiting an inclination toward technological innovation. By doing so, they found their special place, allowing them to collaborate successfully with both generations.

Gen Xers usually distinguish themselves from other generations through their commitment to hard labor. They are often called "lone wolves" because they prefer tackling tasks independently rather than relying on collaboration or group thinking processes. As a result, numerous employers have recognized and commended Gen Xers for their efficiency in the time spent at work and developments achieved instead of participating in staff activities. This dedication is also evident in Gen Xers' ability to remain concentrated on long-term objectives even when there might be temporary disruptions or changes imposed by upper managements.

Gen X also tend to be more receptive to technology than Baby Boomers, while not allowing it to become an overbearing factor like Millennials—they tend to utilize it mostly when necessary. Still, Gen X often feel the need for some novel gadget out there, solely for having's sake, to help them remain up-to-date with trends while maintaining their productivity by investing too extensively in instruments that could make little sense within their particular career role or field. Moreover, Gen Xers tend toward a pragmatic approach when making choices; they deliberate based on what makes logical sense rather than getting immersed in contemporary vogue at any given time or following unanimous opinion unthinkingly and lacking consideration of past factual information first.

Challenges and Opportunities for Gen X in the Modern Workforce

As Gen X enters a highly dynamic job market, they face the challenge of remaining competitive within such an environment. Given that the emergence of new technology has drastically altered many industries, Gen Xers must actively seek ways to distinguish themselves from other generations regarding their pursuits for employment opportunities along with career growth possibilities.

There is one strategy by which Gen Xers can denote themselves—focusing on leveraging their technological experience and knowledge to make them stand out amongst other applicants or competitors. Given that older generations may not be accustomed to the most recent technology, Gen Xers can use their understanding to ensure that they remain ahead of the competition when seeking jobs or promotions within their current company. Moreover, Gen Xers should concentrate on evidencing how they have adjusted over time while still taking advantage of conventional abilities gained during their professional lives. By undertaking such steps, Gen Xers can demonstrate an aptitude for keeping up-to-date without sacrificing any valuable experience collected in former times.

Gen X also has many chances available when searching for work or aiming to further their career. For instance, many employers perceive multi-generational teams as beneficial as diversity brings together varied viewpoints, leading to more imaginative answers to the problems businesses face today. Additionally, with numerous Baby Boomers retiring shortly, there will be an abundance of roles being opened at every level in corporations, which provide incredible opportunities for experienced Gen X professionals who are on the lookout for new experiences in the labor force and desire a chance at senior management positions that have been previously held by Boomers before them.

Gen X has a distinct advantage in understanding customers' needs due to growing up during a period wherein consumer preferences were rapidly changing owing to simultaneous advances in technology and globalization, making them ideal for working in customer service roles that require understanding generational trends (e.g., marketing or sales positions where understanding customer behavior across different age groups is critical).

Gen Xers face obstacles as well as numerous opportunities that are associated with belonging to their demographic group. They should utilize traditional skill sets and modern technological capacities while taking advantage of potential openings from increased retirements among Baby Boomers. By doing so, Gen X professionals can enjoy successful careers despite stiff competition from younger Millennials entering the workforce and older generations leveraging their experience and ancient practices.

Implications for Organizations and Managers

Organizations and managers must know the distinctions between Gen Xers (born 1965-1980) and other generations to maximize their potential. An essential contrast to note is that Gen Xers are more self-governing than different generations, often preferring to work independently or in small groups rather than large teams; as such, employers should grant Gen Xers the independence they need to prosper.

Another critical differentiation is that, as opposed to process, Gen Xers prioritize outcomes when making decisions. Gen Xers focus on short-term goals and tangible outcomes rather than long-term planning or abstract concepts. Consequently, organizations should establish clear expectations for performance, while granting Gen Xers the freedom to devise creative solutions for achieving these targets.

Given their experiences with economic strain, rapid technological change, and political upheaval growing up, Gen Xers are considerably more suspicious of authority figures than other generations, such as Millennials or Gen Z. Managers should thus anticipate a degree of resistance from Gen X regarding decision-making or policy formulation; however, if appropriately managed by leaders who appreciate what motivates them and understand their needs, this resistance can result into improved communication and problem-solving skills.

Unlike some other groups, such as Millennials and Zoomers, who prioritize adventure over stability where career decisions are concerned, Gen X tend to value job security over career advancement opportunities. Therefore, corporations may need to adjust benefit packages to have an attractive appeal for Gen X workers whose topmost priority remains to guarantee protection against terminations due to employment insecurity concerns.

4

Understanding the Multi-Generational Workforce

The workplace is transforming. Nowadays, the complexity of having multiple generations working together within an organization and creating multicultural and dynamic work settings are becoming increasingly more commonplace. Such situations entail varied intergenerational difficulties, such as age segmentation and generational discrepancies, which need to be better comprehended for employers to capitalize on the advantages they bring. This chapter explores all elements constituting a multi-generational workforce and how organizations can utilize diversity to become more successful establishments.

Defining the Multi-Generational Workforce

The multi-generational workforce is an integral component of the contemporary workplace, encompassing diverse ages and levels within any institution, ranging from young Millennials at the outset of their career path to experienced Baby Boomers. Every generation brings distinct values, backgrounds, and perspectives that can positively influence an organization's success.

Within an organization, there could potentially be five separate generations employed concurrently—each with its own set of values and beliefs regarding work culture and anticipation of success. Given the growth in the number of new generations entering employment, organizations must comprehend how these generations interact differently with technology and with other age groups.

One way this can be done is by defining what a multi-generational workforce looks like when put into practice. A multi-generational workforce encompasses personnel from all generations currently active: Gen Z (born 1997–2012), Millennials (born 1981–1996), Gen X (born 1965–1980), Baby Boomers (born 1946–1964) and Traditionalists/Silent Generation (born 1925-1945). There are variations between generations when it comes to the use of technology. For example, while Gen Z may be well-versed in modern technology and competent enough to utilize it for everyday operations such as communication or project management, Baby Boomers might prefer more conventional face-to-face interactions or paper documentation instead of digital ones. Therefore, organizations must consider these disparities when formulating policies around tech utilization inside a company or devising internal systems to assist employees in completing their duties expeditiously and successfully.

Moreover, organizations should acknowledge that each generation has its benefits and disadvantages when fulfilling day-to-day responsibilities, and comprehending how these can be taken advantage of is fundamental for creating effective teams across different age groups. To illustrate this point further, Millennials usually flourish at multitasking, whereas Baby Boomers have experience handling extended projects; appreciating these differences will help encourage cooperation amongst various ages by making sure everybody feels valued regardless of what life stage they are currently experiencing or the career path they take up.

Generations in the Workplace

The topic of generations in the workplace has recently elicited much consideration. As the labor force progresses, grasping the distinctive generations that form this varied collection is becoming increasingly essential. Every age presents its perspectives, abilities, and principles, which can be taken advantage of for the profit of all involved parties.

Baby Boomers, between 1946 and 1964, are often characterized by their strong commitment to work combined with an appreciation for things such as loyalty, esteeming others highly, and hardworking attitude—qualities that remain extremely valuable in any organization at present times. Baby Boomers bring forth experience and knowledge accumulated from their many years in the workplace. Furthermore, they manifest a desire for stability on the job.

Gen Xers, born between 1965 and 1980, possess deviating values compared to prior generations, predominantly due to technological advances that emerged during that era. As such, Gen Xers are more inviting toward change and tend to seek out flexible scheduling or telecommuting opportunities while still maintaining punctuality when it comes to results yielding performance. Their attitude makes them ideal candidates for contemporary workplaces, which often embrace varying conditions.

Millennials, born between 1981 and 2000, constitute a crucial component of contemporary workforces due to their mastery of technical abilities, global outlooks, and entrepreneurial attitude.

These qualities allow organizations to ascend toward more tremendous domestic and international success. Millennials also bring novel approaches to businesses via creative problem-solving methods that often result in ingenious solutions that may have yet to be discovered by other generations with more expertise.

Lastly, Gen Z (born after 2000) is beginning to enter the workforce, bringing digital fluency and an appreciation for diversity, openness, collaboration, technology usage awareness, mental health consciousness, and sustainability initiatives. With their distinct viewpoints, they will undoubtedly continue reshaping present protocols within both large and small organizations.

Leaders must recognize and value these distinctions among various generations within their organization so they can tap into collective strengths and form possibilities for improvement. Managers can foster involvement across all company layers by issuing pertinent feedback and furnishing employees with applicable development options, taking it toward more significant achievements.

Baby Boomers (Born Approximately 1946-1964)

The Baby Boomer generation, born between 1946 and 1964, consist of one of the four generations currently in the workforce. With an entrepreneurial mindset and a wealth of experience, they are often deemed invaluable to any business environment. A key advantage associated with this cohort is that they typically demonstrate a strong commitment to fulfilling job roles, thus making them highly dependable personnel who can be trusted implicitly.

Baby Boomers are known to be dedicated and committed employees, which makes them more likely to remain with a company for extended periods. Baby Boomers provide businesses with more excellent continuity than other generations. Furthermore, due to having been through multiple economic cycles during their career lifespans, Baby Boomer workers possess an understanding that helps them make sound decisions in volatile conditions. Another benefit of employing Baby Boomer staff is that they can offer strong leadership abilities based on years of experience in managerial positions. Even though younger generations may find it hard to develop such skills without similar life experience, businesses can still count on experienced Boomer leaders who have already been confronted with complicated decisions or complex issues.

Moreover, Baby Boomers generally have good relationships within their community as they are frequently involved in activities even after retirement or accepting part-time work arrangements and consulting roles beyond their primary job. Therefore, companies can take advantage of those networks if needed for supplementary resources or possibilities through mentorship programs and collaborations, which could be advantageous and help unite diverse age groups.

Gen X (Born Approximately 1965-1980)

Gen X is often portrayed as the "forgotten" generation between Baby Boomers and Millennials. Although those belonging to Gen X are now firmly in their mid-to-late 40s and 50s, they remain an indispensable part of today's multi-generational workforce. Despite being associated with greater job satisfaction than Millennials, organizations may face specific difficulties when attempting recruitment, retention, or management related to Gen Xers. Though typically seen as independent thinkers who welcome autonomy while undertaking work responsibilities, Gen Xers may experience feelings of neglect or inadequacy if their contributions go unnoticed or unrewarded.

Compared to Baby Boomers, which prioritized loyalty most, Gen Xers attach greater importance to flexibility. As such, Gen Xers may only be as willing to stay with an organization for extended periods if their achievements are acknowledged or there is no possibility for career advancement. To ensure these personnel remain engaged within a company over an extended period, the company should provide competitive salaries, reward their efforts, recognize accomplishments, offer regular training sessions, and encourage genuine collaboration among business divisions.

In terms of recruitment efforts, Gen Xers may not be as technologically proficient as Millennials; thus, traditional methods such as print advertising should be used with digital media campaigns to attract these individuals into one's organization. Furthermore, it could prove beneficial for employers looking to hire Gen Xers from outside the industry to direct their attention toward how the individual's background will bring fresh perspectives rather than underlining how much experience they have within a specific field, given that this generation is likely more appreciative of novel ideas over entrenched processes or experiences. Regarding performance management strategies that resonate among Gen X employees, they tend toward regular feedback sessions instead of annual performance reviews, which can aid in maintaining high morale while guaranteeing that expectations remain clear within the team dynamic.

Millennials (Born Approximately 1981-2000)

Millennials are integral to any multi-generational work environment, bringing forth values, perspectives, and experiences that can profoundly benefit businesses. Millennial workers appreciate transparency within the workplace where open discussions regarding company objectives, policies governing decision-making processes, and other matters relating to employee engagement occur freely. It is pertinent for employers to invest the requisite time in understanding their motivations, behaviors, and working style.

Millennials tend to choose a flexible working schedule to achieve an equilibrium between their professional and personal lives and are often perceived as having a solid faith in the potential power of technology and social media, which is evident in how Millennials approach their work. Rather than traditional methods such as emails or phone calls, they are more likely to use digital tools like Slack and Zoom to collaborate with colleagues and rely on mobile devices for communication.

Millennials who have experienced the heightened globalization of recent decades and encountered numerous diverse cultures are inclined to show an appreciation for different backgrounds. Employers should leverage this opportunity to promote inclusion within their workforce. Millennials are driven by a robust value system that originates personally and from ethical standards regarding diversity initiatives implemented at companies they work with.

Lastly, employers must be aware of certain expectations held by Millennials regarding compensation packages; even if these expectations may not always be confessed publicly, recognition for hard work is still significant for members of this generation.

Hence, businesses need to find innovative methods to recompense employees without exceeding budgets while simultaneously assuring competitive pay rates according to market norms.

Generation Z (Born Approximately 2000-2012)

Gen Z is the most recent demographic to enter today's workforce, and they are often referred to as digital natives due to their aptitude for technology and preference toward digital media. Gen Z inclines job security rather than career growth, making them a good fit for various organizational roles. Additionally, this group boasts diverse capabilities, typically displaying creativity and technical expertise, which makes them valuable team members.

One of the most prominent benefits attributed to Gen Z is their capacity for creative reasoning, which can be advantageous to enterprises seeking imaginative solutions that could have gone unnoticed. Gen Z offers valuable insight into leveraging technology to heighten effectiveness and augment customer service. Companies need to comprehend Gen Z's one-of-a-kind outlook on life to reach out to this group more proficiently and construct a work atmosphere where everyone feels appreciated and considered.

Gen Z employees are known to prioritize work-life balance over other generations, which is why employers must provide flexible options when it comes to scheduling and workloads. To attract Gen Z workers, organizations should offer opportunities for remote working or flexibility about when tasks should be accomplished within a given day or week.

Furthermore, employers should consider incentives such as performance bonuses and additional vacation time to motivate Gen

Z workers and guarantee that all voices are heard during meetings or brainstorming sessions. Comprehending Gen Z's preferences will assist managers in effectively managing this cohort while fostering a workplace culture that encourages diversity and ingenuity among every generation employed by any organization.

Conflicts Arising from Generational Differences

Recognizing the conflicts arising from generational differences is essential to ensure a productive workplace. Such tensions can result in decreased productivity and dissatisfaction, necessitating employers to identify each generation's strengths and weaknesses and individual needs and perspectives. Businesses must recognize that every age comes with values, experiences, attitudes, and expectations.

Employers must consider several key differences when it comes to the various generations in the workforce. For instance, Baby Boomers generally prioritize career advancement, whereas Gen Xers tend to value flexibility. Millennials seek meaningful work with purpose, and Gen Z workers typically look for feedback about their performance. An understanding of such dynamics can assist employers when creating policies that address different generational needs.

Another critical factor in managing generational differences is communication; each generation has its preferred mode of dissemination, which could be anything from face-to-face conversations to digital communicative methods like email or text messaging. Employers need to create transparent pathways of communication that honor everybody's preferences so that all personnel feel listened to and respected in the workplace.

Furthermore, as much as feasible, employee improvement plans must consider generational distinctions; devising customized educational opportunities based on each employee's experience level could aid in guaranteeing that everyone feels involved with their job assignments and sustained by their co-workers throughout generations.

Providing adaptable work arrangements such as distant working selections or flexible hours can further assist in addressing different ages' necessitated balance between professional life obligations and personal life commitments without detrimental effect on productivity or efficiency levels at the office. Ultimately, stimulating intergenerational mentoring programs tend to be advantageous for knowledgeable employees who desire to pass down knowledge and younger workers who crave advice from someone more experienced than them in specific fields.

Collaboration Opportunities from Generational Differences

Today's multi-generational workforce is one of history's most assorted and dynamic talent pools. Every generation contributes distinctive capabilities, outlooks, and ideals to their workplace settings. One significant advantage of having a diverse mixture within the workspace is allowing for collaboration between generations. By bringing different ages together, they can share thoughts and work cooperatively toward achieving novel solutions for existing issues.

Millennials may bring their unique technological skillset to the table to assist older workers in becoming more knowledgeable about technology. At the same time, Boomers can provide mentoring and counsel on navigating complex customer service or office politics. By combining the different strengths of each generation, organizations can reach better results than if they only trustingly rely on one group alone. Therefore, generational diversity can significantly contribute to furthering an organization's development by offering increased cultural awareness training and a heightened level of cultural intelligence among the staff members. This understanding can provide organizations with the insight to comprehend better how members from differing backgrounds perceive matters such as gender equality or racial equity, which may ultimately lead to a more equitable working environment whereby everyone is respected and valued regardless of their age or background. Moreover, this allows for potential opportunities wherein diversified teams boasting distinct abilities are assembled to bring forth solutions fittingly suitable for addressing today's intricate business dilemmas, issues that only some people likely have all the answers to resolve alone.

Flexible Work Arrangements

The present-day labor force is comprised of multiple generations from Millennials to Baby Boomers. Every generation brings distinctive values, preferences, and expectations into the workplace. Employers should consider providing flexible working arrangements to comprehend the multi-generational workforce effectively and establish an integrated workplace environment. Flexible working arrangements may extend from changed timetables to telecommuting or job-sharing opportunities that offer employees enhanced authority over their schedule and more time for family commitments and personal obligations.

Flexible work arrangements are advantageous not only to employees but also employers. Flexible working options can result in heightened morale as workers perceive themselves as valued by having the latitude required for better managing their lives outside office premises. Furthermore, offering flexibility is likely to bring about higher engagement degrees, which could eventually result in improved productivity and steadfastness among team members. Flexibility must also be considered when engaging younger workers who have been exposed to technology-driven lifestyles offering more freedom than the traditional nine-to-five job in terms of autonomy and potential for professional growth within a company's structure.

Employers must carefully evaluate all possible outcomes before introducing any changes throughout their organization or departments to avoid universal side effects such as understaffing issues and disparities among team members because of depleted resources caused by employee absences during specific time frames. In addition, firms must establish impartial policies across various generations, ensuring everybody experiences respect while simultaneously taking advantage of these arrangements.

PART II

Gen X Leadership Styles

5

Leadership Styles in the 21st Century

Leadership is an ever-evolving capability, and knowledge about the transformations and subtleties in modern leadership dynamics is essential to stay ahead of the competition in the 21st-century workplace. In leadership, tactics can assist in creating strong teams, enhance productivity, and supply executive coaching to optimize performance. Regardless of whether one is a new manager or a veteran executive, there are illuminating points for those looking to refine their competencies as leaders during these times.

Autocratic Leadership Style

Autocratic leadership, employed in numerous organizations and ventures, occurs when a leader has absolute authority, allowing them to have supreme control over decision-making without consulting with their team or subordinates. Autocratic leadership can be advantageous when a situation requires swift decisions or when group consensus cannot occur, mainly because it facilitates clear direction from a leader to those they lead, along with supplying expectations that must be met.

The principal drawback of autocratic leadership is the potential for employees to feel resentful or demotivated due to needing more input in decisions being made about them. Furthermore, with this type of direction frequently comes limited chances for creativity and invention, as suggestions from team members are usually not welcomed but instead dictated by the leader exclusively. This overall lack of consideration given to possible alternatives when making choices can often result in expensive missteps.

For leaders to achieve success, they must understand when autocratic leadership will be the most effective and when other methods may prove more suitable, given that granting employees opportunities to explore their capabilities and fostering collaboration between peers have been evidenced to promote productivity within teams and organizations.

Autocratic Leadership styles can still have numerous benefits when used correctly; autocratic leaders must strive to ensure that they provide appropriate guidance and feedback when necessary, throughout the execution of any projects, so that all participants remain focused on the goals and feel appreciated, instead of harboring resentment toward their leader.

However, leaders must rely on other leadership styles as well if a sustained level of success is desired within an organization or team. Therefore, autocratic leadership is just one tool out of many, which leaders should utilize only when it best fits the situation to lead to desired outcomes.

Transformational Leadership Style

Transformational leadership is a form of management that focuses on motivating employees to work hard and attain high performance levels. Transformational leadership operates under the principle that leaders should actively strive for transformation within their teams by inspiring them by example, empowering them with responsibility, and involving them in a unified vision of success. Transformational leaders emphasize teamwork among team members to encourage creativity and originality and inspire those around them to reach their highest potential by providing appropriate assistance.

Transformational leaders are skilled at detecting talent within their teams and effectively utilizing it. Even though they remain conscious of the security of those they direct, transformational leaders do not shy away from confronting notions or taking risks for the benefit of the project. By constructing relationships with every single member of their team, transformational leaders foster trust and develop loyalty among them, permitting everyone implicated to experience sustained support during all stages of development.

Companies worldwide have been forced to make numerous adjustments to remain successful in the 21st century. One such adjustment is how they manage people, as workers increasingly expect more from employers than ever before. A suitable leadership style is required to ensure that all staff members are treated fairly, equitably, and ethically, while being given access to resources needed to reach their highest possible performance levels. As the business world continues to evolve with technology and globalization in mind, transformational leadership is becoming increasingly important for managers seeking to have their teams meet ever-growing demands without compromising morale or product quality.

Given the complexity that modern organizations often face, building an atmosphere where employees feel invigorated while also catalyzed into action has become especially pertinent and necessitates a level of skill only achievable through transformative leaders. Transformational leadership has emerged as an advantageous alternative over other leadership styles, as it creates a supportive and collaborative work culture, resulting in higher morale among staff members. Furthermore, transformation leadership tends to lead to increased productivity across the organization, ultimately leading to overall organizational success.

Servant Leadership Style

While servant leadership has existed since the 1970s, it is becoming progressively prevalent during the 21st century. Servant leadership style occurs when a leader provides services to their team members, helps them toward achieving their goals, and actively seeks to create an environment that makes each member feel valued, respected, and backed up by one another. The servant leader usually puts the needs of those under their guidance ahead of any personal desires that they may have while promoting collaboration amongst all participants to achieve tremendous success as a group.

Servant leadership style emphasizes forming relationships with those being led to engender trust, understanding, and respect between the two parties. The purpose of this methodology is for leaders to assume the role of mentors or coaches instead of bosses or dictators, allowing team members some degree of autonomy while still supplying guidance and assistance when necessary. Servant leaders enable everyone's success by providing resources and instructing them through imparting new skill sets or providing feedback on how they might better their performance. When carried out appropriately, a servant leader can generate trust and loyalty among employees while motivating them simultaneously.

Unlike other authoritative leadership styles, such as autocratic or bureaucratic methods, which focus on command-and-control techniques, servant leadership encourages an open dialogue between leaders and followers so that everyone has input into decision-making processes without fear of reprisal from higher authority figures associated with ranking structures like pyramids, corporate ladders, and pecking orders amongst others.

Evolving Expectations of Leadership in the 21ˢᵗ Century

The 21ˢᵗ century has brought about a rapid change in the world, necessitating that leadership styles keep pace with these changes. Consequently, strong leadership is required more than ever to recognize future trends and make quick decisions in reply to them. Furthermore, comparing expectations of current leaders to those of previous generations reveals drastically different ideals—leaders are no longer expected to be solely authoritative figures who do not take employee needs into consideration; instead, there is an increased emphasis on collaboration to encourage employees while aiding success.

Leaders must recognize that 21ˢᵗ-century teams require more from their leadership than in the past. On top of their traditional leadership needs, teams tend to require leaders who:

- pay attention to their suggestions and treats them with due seriousness.

- make decisions based on data yet are also ready to take risks when required.
- recognize and respect each team member's exclusive expertise.
- promote cooperation instead of rivalry.
- are capable of outlining precise objectives while allowing personal inventiveness during the process for achieving these goals.
- act as both advisor and instructor toward their subordinates.
- engage in the active development of relationships with their colleagues.
- provide honest feedback without any regard for ego or judgment.
- communicate authentically and openly with team members.
- build trust by expressing empathy and compassion as well as respect for different opinions.
- demonstrate fairness when making decisions and acknowledge contributions made by individual team players.

Furthermore, it is essential for leaders to recognize that no two teams are identical, and each team has its exclusive dynamics, necessitating modified leadership strategies. Good leaders must be able to modify their style for each situation that they confront and recognize when a more involved approach would be beneficial or when they should take a step back and grant autonomy to their team. Nonetheless, an ongoing review concerning success stories, along with failure scenarios so errors can be prevented going forward, and a comprehension of how best every individual works together as part of a collective toward attaining common objectives is paramount as we move into another decade ahead.

Synthesis of Leadership Styles

In the 21st century, leadership styles have changed significantly from their historically top-down approach due to organizations' need to remain competitive and pertinent in an ever-changing business environment. Combining multiple leadership styles has become essential for driving organizational success and sustainability.

Leaders today must be able to merge different approaches to manage their teams effectively; additionally, they should possess the capability of recognizing when various scenarios necessitate distinct responses and responding promptly accordingly. Influential leaders must understand the significance of different leadership styles and how they affect team dynamics, productivity, and morale. Furthermore, traditional approaches must be complemented with modern methods, including flat structures, open communication systems, distributed decision-making processes, self-organized teams, and agile methodology to remain competitive. Through such measures, diversity can be embraced, which causes employees to feel valued while simultaneously spurring creativity, leading toward organizational success.

Consequently, no matter what style or approach is chosen, to optimize performance and ensure integrity throughout any endeavor, successful leaders should strive to:

- have a clear purpose and set vision/goal attainment strategies.
- motivate others through engagement and recognition practices.
- develop effective communication and conflict resolution skills.
- understand context to be able to apply the appropriate methods.

Developing 21st Century Leadership Skills

The importance of leadership styles has changed significantly in the 21st century, necessitating different skills. Although traditional leadership roles remain pertinent, contemporary leaders must have the capacity to adjust and confront novel difficulties. Consequently, it is critical for any leader seeking to stay viable in today's ever-evolving business environment to invest in developing modern 21st-century leadership abilities, such as:

- strategic thought processing capabilities to be able to identify issues, formulate suitable solutions, and then implement them successfully with efficacy.

- a deep understanding of present trends and the capability to foretell future ones to succeed.

- innovative strategies that assist their organization in reaching its goals effectively.

- solid communication skills so that their vision and objectives can be relayed accurately to other important stakeholders within the company.

- effective decision-making capabilities, which are essential for any leader wishing to excel at their position.

- ability to assess multiple options and select the one that most effectively meets organizational objectives while minimizing potential risks and associated consequences when presented with complex situations or decision-making processes.

- knowledge on how best to manage resources so that their teams or organizations can reach goals efficiently without compromising the quality of work or making shortcuts on essential projects due to lack of funds or workforce capacity.

Furthermore, 21ˢᵗ-century leaders must remain up to date regarding technological advances and alterations occurring within their industries, to keep pace with industry trends while capitalizing on benefits from emerging technologies like AI and robotics. Given that technology has become a mandatory tool in today's digital economy, it is indispensable that pioneers comprehend how best to use these improvements to maximize the gains resulting from them. The amalgamation of such skills will ensure improved performance among team members, resulting in overall success when applied to any organizational endeavor.

Gen X and Leadership in the 21ˢᵗ Century

Gen X is a generation that has been entrusted with the responsibility of guiding the 21ˢᵗ century. As an interconnection between Baby Boomers and Millennials, Gen Xers bring unique skillsets and experiences to leadership roles. Gen Xers have had to confront many problems, such as a rapid economic transformation, globalization processes beyond their control, and technological progressions leading to new jobs, which molded them to be more prepared than earlier generations to match up with today's everchanging corporate world demands.

As leaders in this new age, Gen Xers must continually assess their strategies and techniques for success. Gen Xers comprehend that accomplishment relies upon how well they can show initiative while stirring others around them. Gen X is more inclined to make the most of information-driven primary leadership forms rather than depending exclusively on instinct or experience when making essential choices.

Furthermore, Gen Xers are renowned for their capacity to think independently and develop new ideas instead of adhering strictly to conventions or practices of older generations. This tendency manifests itself in their willingness to take chances when deemed necessary, as well as their openness toward unconventional methods when required, which separates them from other generations when it comes to leadership approaches found within today's workplace.

Challenges of Leadership in the 21st Century

At present, leaders must confront an unparalleled set of difficulties as they endeavor to lead their teams and organizations. Since the outset of the 21st century, considerable modifications have occurred due to globalization, digital technology exposure, and escalated levels of rivalry that have substantially affected how frontrunners approach their obligations and duties. To be successful in this brand-new environment, 21st-century leaders must possess an acute understanding of the people whom they supervise and trends that could shape them; furthermore, it is essential for leaders to be able to accommodate perpetually transitioning requirements.

At its essence, leadership consists of establishing a common vision shared by team members and stimulating them to collaborate to attain it. However, nowadays, other elements affect successful leadership. One main challenge is grasping how different generations view work divergently; Millennials have different anticipations than Baby Boomers or Gen Xers. Leading figures must recognize these discrepancies and communicate successfully with each generation so that everyone on the crew can strive toward similar objectives. Moreover, though technology may make procedures more proficient within an organization, it could also produce predicaments if not regulated competently. Leaders in the 21st century should understand how technological advances both can help them realize their aims and hinder progress if misused or taken advantage of by employees or customers.

Usage of Technology in Leadership

The 21st century has witnessed a considerable change in how individuals lead, and technology assumes an ever more significant part by enabling better communication, collaboration, decision-making, and problem-solving. Technology enables leaders to access data rapidly and proficiently while furnishing insights into intricate organizational dynamics. Owing to breakthroughs in AI and automation, technology can inspire creativity, enhance cooperation, streamline processes, and increase efficiency.

Leaders are utilizing technology to acquire abilities such as emotional intelligence, which is pivotal for triumphant leadership in the digital age. By using AI-driven tools like sentiment analysis or facial recognition software, leaders can better comprehend their team members' feelings and responses, enabling them to make informed decisions based on the specific needs of each group member. Additionally, technology may be employed for activities aimed at developing teams or virtual meetings, granting remote workers worldwide an opportunity to cooperate on projects without having to traverse extensive distances.

Technology has enabled organizations of whole sizes to become more agile by utilizing cloud computing solutions that allow data access from anywhere at any time in just a few clicks without requiring heavy investments in hardware infrastructure. Cloud-based technology also enables organizations to respond rapidly when confronted by unexpected challenges as they can access resources within minutes as opposed to days or weeks, which would be necessary if using traditional methods such as hardcopy documents stored onsite. Furthermore, cloud-based technologies tend to be more cost efficient by providing businesses with greater flexibility when setting aside resources for new initiatives or projects rather than investing large sums upfront on hardware solutions that may need to be updated within a limited timeframe.

Ultimately, in this current day and age, leadership styles have taken on a far more dynamic, creative, and team-oriented approach. Consequently, executive coaching has become an undeniably helpful resource for those looking to refine their abilities and remain knowledgeable in leadership. An amalgam comprising of modernized and traditional methods is required to provide leaders with a continually developing environment wherein they can drive all present operations forward.

6

The Gen X Leadership Approach

As the world of leadership continues to evolve, Gen Xers are leading the charge with an approach that is both adaptive and pioneering. As Millennials become more entrenched in management roles, it is essential for Gen Xers to adjust their leadership style to attract the younger generation. Through comprehending intergenerational intricacies at play, experienced and knowledgeable individuals can construct effective strategies to better guide their teams toward success.

Introduction to Gen X Leadership Traits

Gen Xers are well known for being independent and practicing a healthy work-life balance. At the same time, their innovative problem-solving aptitude provides them with a greater focus on results. Regarding leadership traits, Gen Xers have been characterized as highly versatile leaders with an uncanny ability to adjust quickly even under altering conditions and manage various people simultaneously without difficulty.

Given that those who possess an analytical mind are typically direct communicators with a propensity toward practical solutions rather than any long-term strategies, Gen Xers are frequently viewed as bridge builders between organizational silos due to their comprehension of how the different departments should be working in unison to obtain success. Additionally, these individuals demonstrate remarkable talent when it comes to maintaining focus on short-term goals while keeping track of any impending long-range objectives at the same time.

Gen Xers prioritize collaboration over competition, making them admirable and loyal team players. Despite this, Gen Xers are willing to act and make difficult decisions when essential. Gen X leaders also find comfort in functioning within unclear circumstances and flourish under pressure because they recognize how important it is for tasks to be finished expeditiously without compromising quality requirements to remain competitive in their respective industries. Gen X leaders bring distinctive capabilities that make them well-suited for any organization seeking creative solutions while preserving elevated levels of productivity and effectiveness, thus rendering them irreplaceable resources within any company presently.

Adaptability as a Key Leadership Trait

At present, it is more important than ever to examine and assess leadership characteristics to locate the most powerful procedures for directing a group or company. One trait that has risen significantly in importance inside the contemporary corporate sphere is versatility. Versatility refers to one's capability to swiftly modify maneuvers or plans based on altering situations or conditions; it is an essential talent for any leader as it allows them to promptly react and competently respond to modifications occurring within their surroundings while keeping their staff focused on accomplishing pre-determined objectives.

Adaptability as a leadership trait necessitates that an individual be open-minded and accept change as integral to success. Leaders who embrace transformation rather than resisting it will guide their teams through difficult times, uncovering imaginative ways around intimidating impediments. Adaptability can also assist leaders in sustaining focus on long-term objectives instead of becoming trapped by short-term issues or diversions when making decisions. An adaptable leader considers all potential alternatives rather than solely depending upon what has been efficacious in the past or what they would like individually.

Gen X's approach toward leadership also stresses collaboration between its members, leading to greater adaptability within an organization. As various individuals have different perspectives on a subject matter, it is easier for novel solutions to be found when more than one individual makes all decisions concerning strategy and direction regarding a project or objective of the company. Furthermore, as everyone feels like they are allowed to express their thoughts during decision-making processes, morale tends to stay high, resulting in teams being more focused without any issues sidetracking them from achieving goals arranged by management groups utilizing this administration model.

Pragmatism: A Practical Approach to Leadership

Pragmatism is a way of leadership that emphasizes practicality and solutions. This approach to leading has grown in popularity as Gen X, the group of people who have entered adulthood during quick progressions in technology and economic instability, begins to mature. Gen Xers' pragmatic outlook toward life can be seen through their command methods, which emphasize solving issues and finding reasonable answers to troubles. Practical leaders assess a situation from multiple perspectives, analyze its advantages and disadvantages, and consider all accessible resources before selecting what would work out best for everybody concerned.

Gen Xers have been raised with technology incorporated into their daily lives, thus making them more amenable to embracing modern methods and technologies for problem-solving than previous generations. This level of comfort with technology equips Gen Xers with the ability to be adaptable when leading a team; they can quickly adjust in the event of new challenges or transformations in business conditions while still emphasizing achieving goals.

Pragmatism allows Gen X leaders to seek out imaginative means of circumventing roadblocks or concocting pioneering procedures that can contribute to business accomplishments while upholding fundamental values such as integrity and respect for people's talents or abilities. Gen X leaders are also aware of the critical part communication takes in successful leadership and thus employ straightforward language when communicating objectives, to ensure that everyone is aware of what needs to be done without being hindered by verbiage or hazy abstractions. Furthermore, Gen X leaders demonstrate considerable skill at creating an atmosphere where personnel feel comfortable voicing their notions without dread of censure; this helps to support joint effort between staff members and establish a pact between administration and workers, which are both indispensable for success under the pragmatic commandment.

Fostering Collaborative Work Environments

Gen X leaders must cultivate an ambiance that encourages collaborative effort and teamwork to foster improved efficiency, morale, and productivity within workplace settings. This type of atmosphere offers advantages for both employees and employers by promoting healthy collaboration among staff members, resulting in greater focus, motivation, and satisfactory products.

To encourage such cooperative climates between colleagues, Gen X leaders should:

- foster open communication amongst all participants.
- provide an environment that facilitates free exchange of ideas without apprehension of being belittled or strongly criticized by others.
- ensure that everyone on the team has equal access to resources so that they possess identical chances of successfully resolving issues and making innovative contributions.

Leaders should also take extra measures to promote transparency about the decision-making process and project design among their members. Each team member must comprehend what is expected of them and why decisions have been made or tasks assigned in a particular manner. Transparency encourages trust among members as they share a heightened understanding of each other's role within the overall framework of the organization, consequently leading to improved collaboration among them.

Moreover, leaders should be committed to creating an atmosphere where feedback is welcomed rather than dreaded; this can be done by holding frequent meetings in which all participants are invited to express their ideas freely without judgment or disparagement from other members. Furthermore, there should not be any prejudgments about who has good concepts and who does not; instead, everyone should get equal consideration during idea-sharing sessions regardless of age or experience level within the company/organization/team itself.

Finally, leaders should always remember that generating collaborative working environments necessitates a significant expenditure of time; therefore, it is important to stimulate such conferences on at least a weekly basis, to afford everyone with opportunities to assess progress and contemplate new strategies as they plan into prospective initiatives taking place.

Balancing Technology and Interpersonal Skills

Gen X leaders comprehend the value of employing technology to boost productivity and innovation. Simultaneously, they understand that achieving victory in today's business climate necessitates a harmony between technological progressions and influential interpersonal aptitudes. Consequently, Gen X leadership is based on discovering an equilibrium between technology and acknowledging the significance of constructing meaningful relationships with team members and other organizational stakeholders for success.

Gen X leaders have come to realize the importance of cultivating strong relationships, as these connections can provide them with access to resources that could aid in making informed and effective decisions when dealing with a business-related matter. Furthermore, they have realized the importance of soft skills such as communication, collaboration, and creativity when successfully leading a group or team. These key components enable Gen Xers to articulate themselves fluidly, cultivate an environment where creative problem-solving is nurtured, and help everyone reach their fullest potential, while simultaneously achieving organizational objectives. Over time, research has demonstrated that this leadership style encourages employee engagement within organizations, leading to positive results for those involved.

Navigating Leadership Challenges: Gen X Perspective

Leadership is a concept that has been constantly developed throughout the years. As the global climate shifts, so does the approach to and opinion of leadership; this holds particularly true for Gen Xers who possess their own distinctive set of experiences that may shape their leadership capabilities. Being able to face up to the trials associated with leading necessitates comprehending how one can concurrently prioritize competing objectives and form bonds with colleagues and customers while maintaining a forward-looking vision and guiding others through it all.

Gen Xers frequently provide valuable viewpoints when participating in these tasks due firstly to their being comfortable exercising control within traditional corporate environments and rapid entrepreneurial ones. Gen Xers are inclined to emphasize collaboration rather than adhering strictly to an authoritative structure, granting each individual a chance to contribute to the decision-making process. Moreover, they are inclined toward openness when considering ideas from younger generations and other cultures; this receptiveness can afford valuable insight that could have otherwise been overlooked.

Gen Xers also typically exhibit comfort with taking calculated risks, which many businesses now depend upon for success, but also possess sufficient wisdom to plan for potential issues before they become problems. Gen Xers have a distinct approach to communication that differs from those of preceding generations; Boomers tend to favor face-to-face meetings or long emails inundated with sophisticated dialect, while Gen X prefers shorter messages transmitted through text or instant messaging, which get straight down to business without any extra details. This directness enables them to prioritize effectiveness in place of the ceremony when it is time for undertaking the tasks at hand.

Ultimately, Gen X leaders are recognized for possessing strong interpersonal skills that facilitate the formation of confidence and encourage positive connections between team members. It serves to ensure that all involved parties strive toward shared objectives despite any conflicting opinions or backgrounds that may have existed at first, thus enabling effective navigation through contemporary leadership predicaments while comprehending various generational perspectives on topics like communication styles, risk-taking behavior, decision-making processes, and so forth in innovative yet productive manners.

Developing Gen X Leadership Traits in Future Leaders

Gen X's approach to leadership is markedly dissimilar from the traditional models of authority. Gen X leaders are more likely to take risks and be collaborative and proactively motivated than their predecessors. Moreover, Gen X has attained a broader range of abilities due to involvement in multiple spheres and an elevated aptitude for technology compared to other generations.

Gen X leadership displays distinct qualities that should be cultivated in potential future leaders. Any leader must be able to think innovatively about problem-solving and decision-making. Rather than counting on conventional solutions or thoughts, Gen X leaders should be motivated to investigate imaginative methods that may bring surprising results. Moreover, they should be receptive to input from other people to acquire new points of view on the best way forward concerning an issue or undertaking. Subsequently, forthcoming leaders must feel comfortable challenging themselves and delving into unexplored areas when needed.

Gen Xers also possess an intrinsic comprehension of technology, which gives them the aptitude to take advantage of digital tools and platforms to make processes within their organizational activities more effective. Future leaders should continue to strive for proficiency and expertise in this area to keep pace with modern trends related to data examination and automation procedures that are revolutionizing many industries.

Lastly, a fundamental attribute for any leader is constructing relationships across different organizational divisions, which Gen Xers have been known to excel at due to their natural interpersonal abilities. Gen X leaders must persist in honing these qualities by connecting with team members consistently through activities like one-on-one conversations or collective gatherings where everyone can deliver thoughts or cooperate on ventures together without feeling intimidated by hierarchical infrastructures inside the working environment. By instituting constructive connections between all levels of personnel, upcoming business directors will be empowered to take calculated risks while still demonstrating regards toward those around them.

7

Leading with Authenticity and Experience

Leadership is a competency that can be cultivated through experience and knowledge. Being an effective leader necessitates being genuine and having the capability to build relationships with one's team to achieve success. Authentic leadership entails leaders accepting their background, conducting themselves with integrity, and demonstrating assurance when leading. Professional expertise is essential in nurturing genuine leadership skills; experienced leaders can better identify potential hindrances beforehand and make decisions based on prudent judgment. Leadership approaches may vary between organizations, but all strive for the same objective of producing a workspace where personnel feel respected, authorized, and committed. Fundamental practices such as frank discussion, exercises that promote mutual trust, and setting precise expectations ensure teams remain fruitful while feeling appreciated. By exhibiting authenticity accompanied by professional insight, businesses can generate space wherein each individual feels like they possess authority, which serves as the basis for productive groups.

The Unique Characteristics of Gen X

Gen X, termed commonly as the "middle child" of generations, comprises of individuals born between 1965 and 1980. Being the generation that succeeds Baby Boomers while preceding Millennials instills them with distinct characteristics that differentiate them from other cohorts. Gen Xers are typified as independent, self-reliant, and resourceful; many experienced growing up in families where both parents were employed, which enabled ease toward making decisions independently. Instead of flashy displays of accomplishment, they prioritize hard labor for success and have demonstrated a propensity toward values being their propelling force rather than outer rewards or commendations.

Gen Xers take pride in the experience and wisdom they have gained throughout their lives, from the rise of technology to economic changes, which have enabled them to develop a heightened capacity for navigating uncertainty with open-mindedness and tolerance; having grown up during an era where diversity was becoming increasingly celebrated, many Gen Xers became more accepting of different backgrounds—a trait that is indispensable today.

Gen X leaders bring unparalleled authenticity not seen among other generations rather than donning airs or acting superiorly. They tend toward humility while leveraging strategic problem-solving skills developed over time from leading teams or running businesses themselves. This combination endows them with the formidable leadership ability of motivating others while always remaining true to oneself that is highly appreciated by employees when making organizational decisions.

Life Experiences that Shape Gen X Leaders

The lives of Gen Xers, born between 1965 and 1980, have been profoundly shaped by the events that they have encountered. As a generation, they are distinguished from all others as being the first to be exposed to an array of new technologies, such as cell phones and internet access, connecting them in ways that had never before been seen. Furthermore, Gen X has faced immense social changes across numerous nations due to geopolitical alterations, like the fall of communism in Europe, which have inevitably affected their existence.

Consequently, Gen Xers have been obliged to hone their ability to think quickly and adjust expeditiously in shifting conditions due to their life experiences. As such, when Gen Xers assume leadership roles, they are likely well-equipped with an astute comprehension of how technology can be used for either benefit or detriment. To illustrate this point more effectively, Gen Xers might understand that the internet is helpful for communication, but they are also aware that vigilance against cybercrime and other forms of exploitation must accompany its use. Consequently, Gen Xers have a more comprehensive perspective regarding acquiring positions at the head of teams or organizations, as they can understand both the inherent rewards and detriments associated with technological advances.

Due to having encountered varied employment cultures throughout their lives, Gen Xers are well-suited both for working alone where self-starting is demanded or within collective setups wherein cooperation plays a vital role. Hence, Gen Xers can rapidly recognize individual strengths amid groups while concurrently coming up with ideas concerning which resources ought to be used so that projects and undertakings conducted by the organization may prove successful. Also, such experience renders them aware of how to devise schemes, likely allowing existing assets to be utilized effectively while still generating outcomes on deadline and below financial plans whenever feasible.

Authentic Leadership: A Deeper Understanding

Authentic leadership, widely employed in the business circle for many years, requires leading with sincerity and honesty while simultaneously providing employees a chance to cultivate their exclusive skills and competencies. Authentic leaders establish trust and respect so that everyone feels secure enough to express themselves freely and build their strengths.

Authentic leaders recognize that each person has different objectives and requirements and thus endeavor to modify their strategy according to every person's distinctiveness. They recognize the potential for someone to be beset by a task and consequently take the time to extend support or give counsel. Furthermore, they demonstrate an appreciation of diversity in all forms, recognizing that it is necessary to build a culture where everyone feels respected regardless of race or gender. At its very crux, authentic leadership entails forming relationships with one's colleagues rather than simply relying on old-fashioned hierarchical structures such as ranks or job responsibilities.

Authentic leadership allows for greater collaboration and open communication between team members, which can help foster better problem-solving skills within teams. It also gives employees a sense of ownership over their work by enabling them to feel that they have input into the decisions made concerning projects or initiatives inside the organization. Moreover, authentic leadership necessitates trust from both sides; it requires faith in the leader and those being directed so that it may be successful in the long term. A leader must listen intently and comprehend different perspectives before making choices; this assists in constructing stronger relationships among colleagues while simultaneously establishing an atmosphere where individuals know what is anticipated of them at work without feeling overly intruded upon. Subsequently, authentic leadership usually results in higher morale amongst team members, less stress overall, and increased inventiveness, productivity, and development.

Case Study 1: Overcoming Adversity to Build Resilient Teams

Leadership is a convoluted aptitude that necessitates steadfastness and the capacity to adjust to ever-altering circumstances. The leader's responsibility is to furnish direction, counsel, and support to their group to empower them to accomplish their objectives. Even so, it can be challenging for pioneers to experience the difficulties that emerge when driving a group through adversity with great accomplishment. *Case Study 1: Overcoming Adversity to Build Resilient Teams* inspects the involvement of one chief who guided his team through a noteworthy move time frame. This case study explores how the leader motivated his team despite external pressure. Moreover, it underlines what others can learn from this story about managing difficult circumstances honestly and graciously. The firm had been running for almost two decades before shifting into a completely different sector, primarily due to its core customer base having undergone specific changes.

Even though these alterations were not under their control, the company underwent severe monetary strain and confrontation from current personnel who were averse to or incapable of accepting alternatives on such an immense scale. It became plain that the only strategy forward for all concerned—administrators and staff alike— was to embrace transformation vigorously, which was troublesome considering the long-term mistrust created by diverse tactics adopted during earlier transitions.

The challenge at hand inspired the leader of our case study to pursue success. The leader and his recently hired senior management team members committed themselves to guiding each person through the transition process with openness and integrity. Primary emphasis was placed on generating trust among all involved so they could work together toward a shared objective. An atmosphere was generated where everybody felt appreciated, respected, and backed up during every stage of their journey, even when things became disconcerting or alien. As a result, the collective succeeded and established solid ties, giving them steadfastness after confronting more obstacles ahead of time.

Case Study 2: Navigating Technological Changes with Wisdom

In the digital age, an unprecedented amount of demand has been placed upon leaders to remain informed on ever-changing technology trends. Although this may present a formidable challenge, executives are also given an exceptional opportunity to illustrate their wisdom and experience by guiding their organizations through these transformations using genuine leadership qualities. As demonstrated in *Case Study 2: Navigating Technological Changes with Wisdom and Experience*, it is possible for individuals to successfully embrace such challenges while exhibiting positive influences within the organization as well.

In this case study, the executive team at a large tech company was confronted with two significant determinations: whether to invest in new software and hardware upgrades and, if so, how much capital they should apportion to each project. The team had to assess the probable returns against the perils of investing in antiquated technology that could become outmoded within months or weeks. Consequently, rather than simply creating arbitrary decisions based on limited data, the executive team considered prior experiences and current market trends before determining.

The team acknowledged that no single individual could possess all the answers. So, they preferred to trust collective wisdom by utilizing internal resources and external experts who could explain which investments would be most profitable over time. Subsequently, their wise decision-making, regarding investing solely where necessary while sustaining agility for any potential need for speedy alteration, illustrates their ability to navigate technological transformation and how knowledgeable executives have recourse to collective intelligence when addressing such complex judgments. By including multiple outlooks from mixed origins, managers can make more enlightened decisions that promote long-term advantages rather than immediate gains.

Case Study 3: Work-Life Balance and Prioritizing Well-Being

As a leader, it is essential to prioritize one's well-being to be effective. A case study of three entrepreneurs who successfully managed their work-life balance is an exemplary model for how successful and sustainable businesses may be created while simultaneously taking care of oneself.

John constitutes the first entrepreneur studied; he works full time during the day and then dedicates his nights to working on his startup project. He has formulated techniques to prioritize tasks effectively to ensure adequate rest each night, facilitating productivity throughout each subsequent day. John has further organized his days to incorporate periodic pauses to sustain vigor and concentration.

On the other hand, Jane successfully maintained work-life equilibrium by entrusting specific tasks to her co-workers. Perceiving that she was unable to tackle all assignments alone, Jane relegated customer service or accounting duties to avail herself time for significantly imperative matters associated with running a business, such as networking or designing marketing strategies.

Sarah, the third entrepreneur, developed a system that allows her to manage her personal and professional lives without sacrificing either. She dedicated specific timeframes for answering emails or arranging calls with clients while ensuring that she could spend quality time with family members and friends. This way, Sarah had enough opportunity to work and participate in leisurely activities without compromising on running an efficient business operation.

The insights provided by these three entrepreneurs offer valuable advice about how successful leaders can attain their objectives while also upholding good health through maintaining a balanced lifestyle between work life and home life.

Lessons for Emerging Leaders

Emerging leaders must take the lead with authenticity and experience. It is important for leaders to remind themselves that everyone must begin somewhere and that it is fine to have only some of the answers. Aspiring leaders should be sincere and genuine about their weaknesses while also being sure of their capabilities. Authentic leadership necessitates discovering a balance between humility and confidence and possessing enough modesty to welcome fresh ideas while still having faith in one's principles and values.

Experience, through both success and failure, is paramount for aspiring leaders, as it allows them to make more informed decisions in the future. Access to this knowledge can help individuals develop into more proficient leaders by offering insight into different perspectives of team members and colleagues, which could prove invaluable when making choices within the workplace or settling disputes. Furthermore, experience allows leaders to hone their communication skills before taking up more prominent organizational roles. Becoming skilled at interacting with others cultivates trustworthiness, understanding, and respect—which are all necessary to succeed in any field.

Lastly, authentic leadership and professional experience are indispensable for producing successful leadership strategies. Experienced leaders realize the importance of using their knowledge and skills to guide those around them advantageously. A suitable leadership style combined with genuine practices can provide an uplifting atmosphere that promotes development, collaboration, and triumph.

8

Balancing Technology and Human Connection

In this modern age in which technology has an all-encompassing presence, it can be challenging to navigate the correct equilibrium between tech connections and meaningful human connections. Gen X is unique as they have experienced both traditional social bonding methods and digital interaction; this allows them to find a way to balance their use of technology with fostering strong relationships, which is critical for attaining well-being.

Gen X's Unique Perspective on Technology and Leadership

Gen X constitutes a distinctly unique population. Having experienced both conventional analog technology and modern digital age technological advances, they possess an intriguing perspective regarding utilizing technology for business leadership. Gen Xers can be distinguished from other generations by their ability to benefit from contemporary digital resources while at the same time maintaining interpersonal rapport with colleagues and subordinates alike.

Regarding utilizing technology for leadership, Gen Xers view it as an addition instead of a substitution for human contact.

They comprehend that while mechanization and AI can help streamline procedures, people are still required to supply feedback, understanding, and guidance to ensure that activities progress efficiently. Additionally, Gen Xers perceive the significance of creating associations through direct communication; this is something that numerous Millennials may need more of owing to their overwhelming dependence on technology for correspondence.

Gen Xers employ technology for leadership by leveraging social media, like Facebook, LinkedIn, or Twitter (X), to establish connections with prospective employees and customers more effectively. Social media allows them not only to form relationships but also to determine the skillsets and interests of others so that they can accurately match individuals with roles within their company or conduct fashion-targeted marketing campaigns based on customer data from these networks. Furthermore, Gen Xers may use video conferencing software to remain abreast of changes about remote teams without neglecting the intimacy that derives from being present face-to-face; this grants them both a means of staying knowledgeable concerning projects while at the same time cultivating strong working associations even when team members are dispersed geographically apart.

Impact of Technology on Human Connection

Gen Xers, born between 1965 and 1980, grew up in a period that witnessed rapid advancements in technology. Computers were increasingly employed across households and workplaces worldwide while the internet was becoming more pervasive. Consequently, modern-day technologies have had an undeniable impact on the way members of Gen X interact with one another. On the one hand, these advances provided them with opportunities to keep abreast of friends and family, through sending emails, engaging via various social media platforms, or resorting to video conferencing toolboxes including Skype or Zoom, among others. Yet, simultaneously, it can be all too effortless for those affiliations to evolve into shallow liaisons with minimal earnest privacy or significance. The difficulty facing Gen X is how they can see both the convenience and hindrance of technology in terms of human bonding. Accomplishing this proficiently necessitates comprehending how technology can genuinely augment relationships, for example, by furnishing us with faster access when we seek aid or affording us more chances than ever for substantive communication. Meanwhile, it is imperative to notice where limits should be set, in which reliance upon "likes" as a substitute for face-to-face discussion could become overbearing.

While there are countless advantages associated with online communication (e.g., having the potential to remain in contact even when one's location may not permit it), there can, unfortunately, exist drawbacks as well (e.g., spending extended periods scrolling on social media and still feeling disconnected). The key lies in achieving an equilibrium between utilizing technology for facilitating interpersonal relationships and preserving a certain level of emotional detachment so that genuine human connection does not suffer due to our unceasing reliance upon gadgets and applications. By effectively recognizing both aspects—how much we benefit from digital correspondence compared to what losses might occur should over-reliance become an issue—Gen X have the capacity to use technological advancements intelligently and acquire all meaningful opportunities available for strengthening authentic human connections provided by contemporary life without exception or exclusion.

Importance of Human Connection in Leadership

In today's technology-driven world, human connection in leadership is often disregarded. Gen X leaders must discover a way to counterbalance the advantages of technology with the value of human association and individual relationships. Technology has enabled us to acquire data rapidly, keep in touch with individuals from everywhere worldwide, and even automate some procedures; however, it ought to maintain the significance of direct interplay and meaningful relationships.

Gen X leaders must recognize the fact that despite their knowledge base having been vastly augmented by technological advances, coming to grips with utilizing this knowledge necessitates formidable interpersonal skills. Forming trust amongst others through meaningful dialogue will be critical for successful leadership. Human connection grants authorities a chance to gain insight into their team members on an intricate level, such as detailing what stimulates and excites them and uncovering strengths and weaknesses, which may help comprehend motivations better when it comes time to make decisions or assign duties.

Furthermore, research has demonstrated that forming human connections can be advantageous for elevating team morale within an organization by creating a climate based on collaboration instead of competition among its personnel. It helps generate a feeling of belonging inside the group, which encourages joint success rather than individual triumph exclusively, thereby producing loyalty toward each other and eventually to the business. Moreover, constructing strong relationships through personal interactions allows for heightened creativity amongst staff members who feel comfortable expressing groundbreaking concepts without apprehension over judgment or criticism from peers or superiors. Unrestricted communication between supervisors and subordinates facilitates invention, resulting in more extraordinary accomplishments for any venture that they engage in jointly as a unit by reinforcing their assurance and making them significantly more productive with tasks that they collectively share.

Strategies for Balancing Technology and Human Connection

Maintaining a healthy balance between technology and human connection could be arduous in the era of social media and smartphones. Gen Xers who are now in their late thirties to early fifties must address this challenge as they try to navigate through two distinct worlds: one composed of traditional manual activities and the other consisting chiefly of digital options. Thus, it is essential for Gen Xers to craft strategies that promote appropriate equilibrium among both realms to keep physical fitness coupled with mental stability under control.

It is possible to manage digital distractions through various approaches. A possible approach may involve establishing firm limits concerning the utilization of technological resources, while another may involve determining boundaries around the use of technology, which could include deactivating notifications or limiting time devoted to devices during portions of a day or week. For instance, some individuals might opt not to employ any tech products after 7 p.m. on weekdays or take a comprehensive 24-hour break from tech every month. Instituting these regulations concerning technological gadgets fosters opportunities for authentic human interaction that are imperative regarding social well-being.

Another tactic is practicing attentive consumption when interacting with online content and social media platforms, such Instagram and Twitter (X). It is possible and important to set intentions when logging into an account, such as:

- only following performances that bring joy and unfollowing those that do not have a positive effect on oneself.
- engaging with posts from people who encourage growth rather than incurring envy or bringing about negative feelings toward oneself.
- taking breaks from scrolling through feeds if being overwhelmed by digital content.

Mindful consumption ensures that digital content does not take control of our lives but instead contributes positively in meaningful ways without provoking harmful emotions within ourselves or others with whom we interact via online means.

Ultimately, Gen Xers should strive to form significant online and offline relationships by devoting quality time to face-to-face interaction through organized collective events like book clubs, recreational sports teams, potluck dinners, or simply spending time with family members, friends, colleagues, neighbors, etc. Establishing these connections enables people to stay linked with their physical environment while giving chances for progressed learning from associates (e.g., cooking classes) or developing compassion via conversations (e.g., discussing recent affairs).

Given that, overall, Gen Xers desire their emotional health and mental wellness in check at this point in life, they must find ways to sustain a substantial equilibrium between technological usage and real-world associations. By instituting device utilization standards, employing mindful uptake, and forming significant bonds outside cyberspace, Gen Xers can accomplish the ideal blend for efficient performance presently and into later years.

Lessons to Learn from Gen X Leadership Strategies

As Gen Xers transition into its mid-life years, Gen X provides critical instruction for subsequent generations. Gen Xers had the benefit of being raised in a period where technology and human association were present; they experienced both elements of this equation. With their background, Gen Xers can draw on technological progress and interpersonal insight when taking charge of teams; they can apportion duties while recognizing how to inspire team members with individual connection and respectfulness.

Gen X leaders understand that there needs to be a balance between managing technology and developing interpersonal relationships on the human level; this approach enables them to establish trust among their team members while maintaining an efficient and effective task-completion process. Furthermore, Gen X leadership strategies often emphasize collaboration rather than competition for teams to reach greater levels of creativity and enhanced productivity, with less emphasis on individual accomplishments or recognition regarding minor successes along the journey.

Gen X leaders have earned a reputation for being more open-minded than their predecessors when considering their employees' work schedules and methods of working. In contrast to preceding generations, who might have been quite strict regarding what are regarded as canonical office hours or procedures, Gen X executives comprehend that affording adaptability can usually result in improved productivity among staff members who perceive value in having permission to conduct duties according to how it is most suitable for them without compromising accuracy or quality norms. Rather than attributing victory exclusively to one individual or organization, success stories are viewed as an overall endeavor contributed by all those taking part.

Navigating Generational Differences

Navigating Generational Differences is no small endeavor. With the entry of Gen X comes a distinct assortment of complications when consolidating technology and human connection. Gen Xers are the first generation to become acquainted with technology from an early age. Yet, they are also a cohort emphasizing face-to-face communication more than any other group. It presents an intriguing predicament for those who supervise and collaborate with Gen Xers as they strive to attain equilibrium between these two arenas.

The key to success in this task is rooted in comprehending each generation's various needs and motivations. It is essential to recognize that even though Gen Xers may be relatively accustomed to technology, they still appreciate personal ties over any other factor. Consequently, those leading a team comprising Gen Xers must ensure sufficient scope exists for practical discussion between personnel and managers alike. Leaders should also consider all communication methods, from verbal to digital, when making decisions.

Moreover, cultivating an atmosphere where open communication is welcomed can influence team spirit and productivity within organizations comprising of Gen Xers and other generations existing in the workplace, such as Millennials or Baby Boomers. When everybody feels listened to by their colleagues and superiors alike, individuals become more involved in their tasks, which culminates in greater job satisfaction overall.

Furthermore, employers should make strides toward recognizing generational discrepancies regarding technological tendencies without disregarding what works best for each setting, mainly when operating with multiple generations under one roof. Acknowledging generational distinction could be beneficial both financially (in terms of increased efficiency) and emotionally (in promoting better teamwork). Ultimately, discovering ways to bridge these gaps will help to achieve harmony between technology usage and human connection, even among different generations.

The Future Landscape of Technology and Human Connection

The Future Landscape of Technology and Human Connection concept is intriguing. With technological progressions, there can be a need for more advancement in technology compared with what level of human connection needs to remain intact. It has mainly been felt by Gen Xers. So many individuals from this era have been responsible for rearing their kids in environments where technological utilization is ubiquitous. The extent to which technology has become absorbed within our lives makes it hard to identify precisely how excessive its use might be when considering both young and grown-ups alike.

The challenge is to find a balance between the appropriate utilization of technology and feeling secure enough in human communication so that relationships can grow instead of diminishing due to the overuse of technology. Various solutions are currently being adopted for linking technology and personal connections, such as using applications like Facetime or Skype for virtual meetings or interactions when physical contact cannot be established. Furthermore, promoting moderation concerning tech usage may help lessen general exposure while still allowing individuals access to utilize requisite tools.

Gen X parents must be aware of how their tech habits influence those close to them, particularly their offspring who have grown up in a world with no other influences except those brought by technological devices and media. It is also crucial for Gen X parents to guide the proper usage levels while concurrently promoting social activities outside the digital space, such as visiting parks or attending family events, without excessively depending on mobiles or gadgets during these trips. Gen Xers can thus demonstrate healthy behavior while spending quality time together without allowing digital screens to overshadow the experience.

In conclusion, technology has revolutionized how Gen Xers interact with one another. Nevertheless, it is fundamental for Gen Xers to remember to bring equilibrium between their tech connection, human bonding, and social interaction. By taking this course of action, Gen Xers can construct dependable relationships and form meaningful connections within the digital age.

PART III

Shaping the Future
of Leadership

9

Gen Xers as Change Catalysts

As Gen Xers enter their prime working years, it is becoming more evident that a shift in leadership is occurring. Millennials have certainly had an impact on social progress; however, Gen Xers are the ones who are proving to be leading agents of change with their exclusive viewpoint, which comes from having experienced both old-fashioned and modern approaches. Gen Xers carry with them a comprehension of how different ages can collaborate to produce meaningful modifications that remain long-lasting. Gen X will likely set up one of society's most noteworthy generational shifts from technological advances to cultural changes.

The Role of Change Agents in Organizations

Organizations have been undergoing continual evolution, necessitating the utilization of change agents to ensure progression. Change agents engender and promote change in organizations by introducing new programs, technologies, or tactics. They abet their peers in understanding the mandatory alterations while also helping them build up novel capabilities and amend themselves according to the changing environment inside an organization. Lately, there has been an augmentation of Gen Xers undertaking said leadership posts as catalysts for transformation.

As a generation raised in an atmosphere of technology and swift social alteration, Gen X possesses exclusive perspectives about how companies must handle changes to remain competitive. Equipped with their talent for bridging the chasm between generations, Gen Xers are prepared to head up organizational transformations successfully and expediently. Gen X tends to have different opinions on what would work best within an organization when administering change initiatives.

Gen Xers are well-suited to leading corporate innovation projects that implement new processes or practices at scale across a large organization's infrastructure. Their comprehensive knowledge of traditional approaches and modern digital trends makes them essential for ensuring successful transitions during organizational transformation while identifying areas where additional support may be required to make the transition as smooth and stress-free as possible. Furthermore, Gen Xers can offer invaluable insight into how organizations need to adjust to keep up with ever-changing market conditions; their understanding of technology enables them to identify better solutions expeditiously while keeping costs low within an organization's budgetary structure, thereby allowing businesses to become increasingly profitable.

Gen X's Skepticism as a Catalyst for Change

Gen Xers tend to be naturally inclined toward skepticism due to the rapid changes that they experienced during their upbringing. This skepticism has enabled them to form robust views on various topics while having sufficient stability in which to do so, thus providing them with an advantageous position as change catalysts. Because of this background, Gen Xers are open to questioning traditional structures or coming up with innovative solutions when necessitated by circumstances.

Gen X's exposure to technology at an early age provides them with a benefit when the digital transformation of their businesses and organizations comes into play. Their technological knowledge and naturally skeptical tendencies make them proficient problem-solvers who can identify solutions efficiently and apply changes that will induce progress. They are often more willing than older generations to take risks, making them suitable for introducing novel ideas or disruptive technologies in otherwise static systems.

The combination of technological understanding and critical thinking skills has enabled Gen Xers to become highly successful change agents in their workplaces and society. It is especially evident when one considers the remarkable number of Gen Xers who have risen through the ranks of top corporations or achieved political success despite making up a relatively small population size compared to other generations. Moreover, due to their unique ability to simultaneously relate with younger and older generations on various topics such as social media trends or technology innovations while still being aware enough about generational differences, Gen Xers are often regarded by many people as "bridge builders" between these two groups. Unlike Baby Boomers, Gen Xers are not accused of being out-of-touch experts from another era.

Robert F. DeFinis, EdD

Gen X's Drive for Innovation

Even though Gen Xers are often overlooked due to being sandwiched between the Baby Boomer generation of greater size and the Millennial generation with higher technological proficiency, Gen Xers have noteworthy roles within the current permanently shifting world. Their exclusive set of capabilities, along with experience, render them prime catalysts for transformation in their organizations.

Gen Xers have been around for a considerable amount of time, allowing them to acquire mastery in various aspects of personal and professional life. This also gives them an edge when attempting to resolve difficulties or concocting novel solutions to obstacles encountered by their companies. Furthermore, Gen Xers can fill any inter-generational gaps due to the insight gained from age-old values and present-day patterns, rendering them highly proficient at aiding firms that wish to innovate while upholding cohesive ties with current practices or procedures.

Gen Xers bring a "can-do" attitude to work that incentivizes others when facing challenging projects or issues. Combining experience, knowledge, and enthusiasm empowers them to implement changes quickly while sustaining quality and precision. Moreover, Gen X understands how significant it is to stay up with technological advances to outpace their rivals while still using time-honored methods when appropriate. Gen Xers employ data analysis tools (e.g., Excel spreadsheets) and leading software applications (e.g., AI chatbots) to complete duties quicker while keeping pace with customer requirements better than ever before. Thanks to Gen Xers' commitment to innovation and their willingness to accept new technologies, companies can gain access to markets that were previously impossible or too expensive to enter.

Positive Transformations Led by Gen X

While Gen Xers are often taken for granted compared to their Millennial counterparts, they have surreptitiously acted as change agents for numerous organizations, promoting beneficial transformations that would otherwise be impossible.

Gen Xers bring a distinct set of capabilities when spearheading changes:

- They possess extensive business knowledge and can comprehend historical situations that prove immensely valuable in determining what direction an organization should take next.
- They tend to be more accepting of risks and flexible enough to adjust quickly, making them an ideal fit for fronting changes within organizations undergoing a speedy transformation in terms of technology or culture.
- They have frequently held positions within the same industry for several decades and thus fully understand how businesses operate from top-to-bottom, allowing them valuable knowledge on tackling transformational projects inside their organizations.
- They possess composure and experience, which can help complement the exuberance and optimism associated with younger generations, such as Millennials or Zoomers, who may need to assess the consequences accurately before taking risks.

The readiness of Gen Xers to take risks makes them effective bridge-builders between disparate generations in the workplace.

This quality is essential for organizations seeking successful transformation programs across multiple departments or divisions. Considering today's technology-driven world and existing economic situation where each dollar matters and success necessitates creative approaches beyond traditional methods alone, Gen Xers can be invaluable resources when it comes to discovering original solutions for corporate complications.

Collaborative Approaches: Gen X Bridging the Generation Gap

As they reach middle age, Gen X has been credited for bridging the gap between the older and the younger. Gen Xers are renowned for their attitude toward connecting generational disparities within companies or organizations by apprehending both sides while simultaneously discovering common ground among them. Gen Xers possess a unique collaborative approach to problem-solving and demonstrate their capability to think beyond conventional resolutions, making them invaluable assets within many organizations striving to attain progressive development.

The distinctiveness of Gen Xers can be primarily attributed to their willingness to collaborate when tackling issues, earning them recognition for finding solutions not limited by conventionality or boundaries. Gen Xers have demonstrated a capacity to gather variant outlooks from all realms of existence to fabricate innovative responses that might not have been considered previously. Furthermore, Gen Xers are inclined to be more receptive than other generations to assume risks and stretch the limits, making them an excellent choice for teams working on endeavors requiring unconstrained thinking or novel methods.

Gen Xers can mediate between various parties, ensuring everyone's perspectives are heard and respected. Moreover, they can draw upon their understanding from multiple industries or businesses to bring fresh ideas into team atmospheres, which aids in continuing projects even when confronted with challenging obstacles. Furthermore, Gen Xers tend to possess a strong sense of responsibility that enables them to stay devoted to long-term objectives despite short-term setbacks or disappointments. As opposed to other generations who may be easily disheartened if plans do not pan out immediately, Gen Xers concentrate on discovering solutions rather than simply giving up due to difficult circumstances; this Gen X trait comes into play significantly as companies persistently strive for triumph over time regardless of what obstructions get encountered along the path.

Leveraging Work-Life Balance Desires for Organizational Change

Gen Xers possess a distinct comprehension concerning work-life balance and organizational alteration. Not only do they benefit from hindsight, but they also understand how companies can be flexible and promptly reply to their employees' needs. While comprehending that attaining equilibrium between working life and leisure is essential to each generation, Gen Xers are uniquely situated to help organizations productively manage modifications while ensuring personnel remain contented yet effective. Consequently, enterprises desiring to stay competitive must recognize this chance presented by these experienced Gen X workers.

Gen Xers have a significant understanding of what it takes to effectuate transformations that give rise to enhanced work-life balance for everyone, ranging from flexible timetables and telecommuting opportunities to bolstered benefits bundles and other worker-centralized initiatives. Moreover, Gen Xers tend to be firm backers of such modifications within their organizations.

Gen Xers' dual roles as purveyors of guidance and catalysts for transition provide them with an unequaled capacity to assist in forming bridges between departments or divisions so that every individual works cohesively toward shared objectives and endeavors more efficiently. They are also readier than their senior counterparts when taking up novel technologies or strategies that could expedite productivity across all spectra. Capitalizing on this experience and willingness toward change presented by Gen Xers permits businesses to lead organizational reconfiguration undertakings through internal aspects, thus ensuring successful outcomes while reducing dissension or opposition to the minimum possible level.

Finally, Gen Xers have had an immense effect on society and continue to act as agents for transformation in the present. They have set a standard of excellence, which has prompted Millennials to strive toward progress. Furthermore, Gen X demonstrates how one generation alone can make lasting changes that will assist in forming a better world for those generations yet to come. In this era where alterations occur across generational lines, it is important to recognize Gen Xers as the catalysts who helped bring about positive developments within societies.

10

Mentoring and Nurturing Young Talent

Gen Xers possess an invaluable combination of life experience and knowledge concerning state-of-the-art technologies, giving them a unique outlook on cultivating, and encouraging young talent. Gen Xers can use their insight to contribute back to society through mentoring and supporting budding skills in those younger than themselves.

Understanding Generational Differences

Careful administration and cultivation of fledgling talent within an organization is fundamental, as it assists in bringing new concepts and perspectives to the surface. Consequently, recognizing generational discrepancies is crucial when guiding this pool of personnel. Generational distinctions are founded on various factors, including age, life experiences, occupational ethos, and values. There can often be noteworthy disparities between Gen Xers and Millennials regarding expectations at the workplace, forms of communication, and professional behavior.

Gen Xers possess more expertise in their chosen fields than Millennials; however, this also implies that Gen Xers might need more insight concerning specific digital trends or technologies, impeding quick adaptation. While Gen Xers are characterized as independent personalities, Millennials prefer collaborative efforts but need more experience to ensure efficient management of complex endeavors and tasks. For instance, even though Millennials usually demonstrate more advanced technical proficiency than Gen Xers, they would be facilitated by being exposed to Gen Xers' principles, such as goal setting and personal accountability, typically obtained through increased experience within an industry or field. For successful mentoring of employees from various generations, leaders and managers alike need to discern what each age group contributes in terms of weaknesses and strengths so that workers can be fostered professionally and be provided with adequate support throughout an organization's lifespan.

Benefits of Mentoring Young Talent

Given that mentoring and nurturing young talent is integral to any organization's success, implementing a mentoring program in the workplace is beneficial for organizations. By offering guidance and assistance, mentors can aid younger employees by developing skills that will benefit them as they progress through their careers. Additionally, forming a successful mentor-mentee relationship could increase loyalty between both parties, uplifting overall team morale.

One of mentorship's most substantial advantages is knowledge transfer across generations. Gen Xers possess knowledge and experience in their respective fields, offering invaluable insight to younger talent that cannot be sourced elsewhere. From technical advice on how best to utilize tools or software applications to more general counsel related to negotiating corporate politics, Gen Xers are well-positioned as advisors due to the wisdom and experience that they have accumulated over many years. By applying this guidance toward their professional development endeavors, mentees can make knowledgeable choices concerning what steps should be taken next in pursuing career objectives.

One significant advantage of having Gen X mentors is their ability to add perspectives from different generations into discussions and decisions revolving around organizational goals or strategies. Thanks to their experience, they can provide a unique perspective that may trigger potential solutions not initially considered by younger members of an organization. Exposure to these distinct viewpoints also helps young professionals become more adaptive problem-solvers who understand how age dynamics influence organizational decision-making.

Experienced mentors offer one-on-one coaching sessions, providing feedback in a safe environment, to encourage open dialogue between both parties and promote trust while ensuring each person's voice is heard fairly and objectively. Ultimately, such relationships boast growth opportunities for all involved as they provide a secure atmosphere conducive to learning, reflecting on experiences, testing ideas, and exploring personal development prospects.

Strategies for Effective Mentoring by Gen X Leaders

Mentoring and nurturing young talent with the help of Gen X leaders is an essential responsibility. Requiring time, effort, and expertise to ensure that subsequent generations are adequately groomed for their prospective societal roles involves dedication. Gen X leaders possess a singular capacity to bridge the distance between seasoned professionals and those just beginning, as they comprehend what it takes to thrive in today's world and can offer invaluable guidance to those wishing to harness the utmost of their potential.

When mentoring young talent, Gen X leaders should be taking a thoughtful approach. Rather than merely providing direction or advice, they should invest in helping everyone develop professionally by considering their unique skills, abilities, and future goals. Thereupon, they ought to devise a plan that will assist them in attaining optimum potential while still offering guidance when required during this process.

Furthermore, Gen X leaders must concentrate on constructing an environment where younger experts can voice themselves freely and take risks without dread of inability or censure from colleagues or bosses. This kind of atmosphere stimulates inventiveness while permitting persons to benefit from errors sans feeling abashed or disgraced.

Trust must be present between mentors and mentees if any real progress is to be made toward meeting the objectives set forth by both parties involved in a mentorship relationship. Successful mentors always seek open communication with their protégés, as it furnishes each party with greater insight into the other's view on an issue, encouraging more productive discussion. This connectivity, which may come through face-to-face meetings, virtual conferencing, email correspondence, text message exchanges, or telephone conversations, gives those engaged in mentor relationships enhanced opportunities for advancement as it helps to build associations upon mutual esteem.

Bridging Generational Gaps

Mentoring and cultivating young talent are an undertaking that presents a significant challenge in the present day. The influx of Gen X into the workforce has made bridging generational divides even more essential. Gen X brings extensive experience and many lessons learned over their lifetimes, which can prove advantageous for younger generations just beginning their careers.

Gen Xers have much wisdom that they can share with Millennials, such as how best to progress through a continually shifting workplace or knowledge to deal adeptly with difficult conversations or complex projects. Gen Xers possess firsthand knowledge of the numerous developments recorded during their time as labor force members, which renders them invaluable resources for more youthful personnel endeavoring to acquire what is necessary to thrive within today's business setting. Gen Xers can provide insight into how various eras think and act differently and thereby assist in forming a bridge between any potential conflicts amongst generational groups. By investing effort into coaching and nurturing burgeoning staff from different generations, employers create an atmosphere where everyone feels accepted without regard for age or level of experience.

In addition to fostering respect within a team setting, mentorship programs bolster employee engagement by supplying personnel with an impetus for helping others realize success. Such mentoring initiatives enhance employees' experience and foster robust corporate cultures, resulting in greater productivity throughout all business operations. While older generations are being overlooked at work partly due to outdated prejudices, Gen Xers possess exceptional wisdom and life lessons, critical for bridging intergenerational divides inside any company.

Knowledge Transfer and Skill Sharing

It is paramount for Gen X professionals, especially those in leadership positions, to prioritize knowledge transfer and skill sharing to mentor and nurture young talent and ensure that future generations are provided with the necessary skills required for success in this day and age. While knowledge transfer can take many shapes, it usually entails transferring information or learning gained by one entity or individual to another person(s).

A Gen Xer may pass on their experience in sales management or software development to a younger colleague who is just beginning to explore these fields. In the same way, an experienced leader could share their knowledge of organizational dynamics and strategic planning with emerging leaders within a company. Through this knowledge sharing, both parties gain more insight into their specialized areas while forming meaningful work connections.

Skill sharing brings the concept even further by permitting individuals to acquire knowledge from each other's experiences instead of exclusively depending on teachings provided by more experienced coaches and instructors. In this kind of learning atmosphere, older professionals can share strategies and advice that have been fruitful for them. At the same time, junior employees obtain practical experience with direct guidance from their colleagues who are already familiar with working within those arenas.

This type of mutual learning allows both sides to gain significantly by cultivating their distinct skills while forming solid ties, which will be highly beneficial further down the line when they look for other job opportunities or collaborate with like-minded professionals in different industries worldwide. By adding knowledge transfer and capacity-building initiatives into mentorship programs intended for Gen Xers, businesses can create an atmosphere where younger generations have access to essential resources that give them a jump start without relying solely on classic methods such as textbooks and lectures. With guidance from experienced veterans, young talent can acquire all the necessary tools and thus spend less time worrying about what lies ahead and focus more on mastering novel concepts instead.

Measuring the Impact of Gen X Mentoring

Gen X is most notably seen as a bridge connecting Baby Boomers with adults of Millennial generations due to holding qualities from both groups. Nonetheless, it has become increasingly acknowledged that Gen Xers possess distinctive traits that can be tapped into to aid upcoming talent in reaching their maximum capabilities. One approach for doing so is via mentorship programs designed mainly to cater to those within this demographic cohort.

Mentoring programs specifically for Gen Xers offer multiple advantages compared to traditional mentoring relationships, as they allow mentors to utilize their own experiences to make a more substantial influence on the lives of their mentees. A mentor who has gone through outstanding achievements and difficult times while forging ahead can grant valuable advice regarding how best to pass through complicated circumstances while keeping sight of long-term objectives. Moreover, such an individual can also provide helpful counsel for proficiently managing time to optimize productivity and harmony.

Furthermore, mentors possessing many years of experience can impart wisdom about approaching office politics—which younger employees might still lack exposure to—along with other indispensable skills like networking and leveraging personal links—all essential tools for success regardless of industry or job position. In addition, experienced Gen X professionals could lend support when negotiating salaries by providing guidance based on decades spent occupying assorted roles at different companies or institutions.

Lastly, the benefits of providing mentorship and nurturing opportunities for young individuals from Gen Xers are undeniable. Mentorship provides valuable learning opportunities to prepare younger generations for their future careers and enables Gen X to stay abreast of current trends and potential job prospects in the market. Through such efforts, mentors can assist in fostering development by granting guidance, giving advice, and offering support, which will also aid them in building the necessary competencies that lead to success.

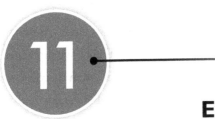

Evolution of Gen X Leadership

The present-day workforce is distinct from what it was a decennium ago, and the appearance of Gen X leaders has altered our contemplation of authority in the work environment. As Gen Xers take up positions as supervisors, they bring talents and viewpoints that assist in forming the future of employment and shift their leadership by shifting labor force movements; this shift in leadership style has implications for companies presently.

Gen X Leadership Characteristics

Gen X is recognized for their particular way of leading. Unlike Baby Boomers, who often appear more old-fashioned, Gen Xers demonstrate distinctive qualities that make them stand out from what came before. Typically speaking, Gen Xers are independent and autonomous beings whose primary focus lies in collaboration and open conversations. Furthermore, they are willing to take risks and introduce inventive solutions when faced with difficulties. Rather than merely obeying instructions without comprehending why they are essential, these individuals focus on efficacy and originality.

The methodologies used by Gen X in leadership have been formed through the alterations experienced within work environments over the past. Given the rapid progression of technology, Gen X has had to accelerate their adaptation to remain on track. They have discerned that operating as a team can be highly beneficial when discovering novel solutions, and they recognize the worth of diversity within such groups. As a result, many Gen Xers now occupy positions with increased responsibility in organizations where they can contribute their distinctive approaches to solving problems.

Gen Xers' influence on workplace culture is particularly noteworthy given their capacity to develop an atmosphere where everybody feels valued and appreciated regardless of age or experience, thereby enabling staff collaboration while preserving high productivity levels.

The Changing Workforce

In the past decade, there has been a drastic alteration in the composition of the workforce. As technology and globalization have become more integrated into our lives, demographics, skillsets, and employee expectations within industries have evolved significantly. Subsequently, traditional ideas surrounding having a typical nine-to-five job no longer necessarily apply; instead, workers are entering arrangements that include flexible hours or even working remotely with increased frequency. This shift has also affected current approaches to leadership taken by organizations throughout all sectors today.

Gen Xers increasingly occupy senior positions in many companies and organizations, with their influence only increasing as more Millennials enter the workplace. Gen X leaders bring unique values that separate them from those who have come before: they demonstrate openness toward change and new ideas, focus on collaboration, commit themselves to life-long learning, comprehend global trends, embrace diversity, use technology for innovative purposes, etc.

Gen X leaders have proven their aptitude in managing today's ever-evolving workplace by considering the distinct needs of employees (e.g., career growth and training). This leadership style acknowledges the considerable worth possessed by everyone within an organization, allowing them to make meaningful contributions that may be achieved through giving direct feedback or implementing new operations.

Gen Xers have also significantly impacted work functioning, introducing fresh technologies such as social media channels and cloud computing services, which enable more efficient collaboration among personnel from various locations worldwide. On top of this, they recognize how essential it is for businesses to maintain a level of agility so that any arising changes can be promptly adapted to.

These unique abilities that Gen X brings to the table accentuate why possessing generational diversity within administration teams remains integral if any corporation wishes secure success in this increasingly competitive modern era that we are currently living in.

Anticipated Shifts in Leadership Approaches

As the world develops and transforms rapidly, so do the desires for leadership in business. Gen Xers have taken part substantially in this transformation, as their one-of-a-kind points of view on work and life have made them priceless to an ever-evolving workplace. It is necessary to contemplate how they are prone to meeting management challenges down the line.

Gen Xers will take on significantly more responsibility and authority regarding leading teams and assume a more significant part in creating strategies for success or giving input regarding decision-making processes. They are also likely to become more accustomed to delegating tasks and accepting different roles within the structure of a team, facilitating them to turn into highly proficient leaders altogether.

Furthermore, Gen X leaders are expected to emphasize collaboration instead of rivalry between people or departments, and thereby transition from traditional top-down methods of leading teams to one that emphasizes empowering employees at all organizational levels. This change could be manifested through increased focus on communication and brainstorming among group members rather than exclusively depending on individual performance metrics or personal opinions when making decisions.

This collaborative approach may lead to amplified innovation within teams due to greater diversity in thought between its members; this tends to improve outcomes and heighten production for organizations as more robust relationships are cultivated between personnel across departments while providing individuals with self-growth opportunities.

Balancing Work-Life Integration

Gen X leaders face the challenge of establishing an equilibrium between work and life in contemporary workplaces. Gen X is frequently viewed as a connection between Baby Boomers and

Millennials; however, while Gen Xers usually demonstrate a composite system combining traditional values and progressive perspectives, their approach to leadership stands apart from both. They comprehend that for firms to retain profitability, they must welcome changing personnel demographics while creating conditions where employees can prosper.

Gen X leaders are adept at generating creative solutions that benefit all those involved in the workplace. This generation of leaders recognizes that for employees to be productive and engrossed, they must have flexibility and support; thus, Gen X leaders focus on fostering trust among teams by providing open communication channels and forming an inclusive environment where everyone feels appreciated. Also, Gen Xers make it a point to ensure that each member has access to the necessary resources needed to flourish within their role while still being mindful of every individual's unique talent or proficiency inside the company.

Gen X tends to keep its sight fixed on long-term objectives while prioritizing short-term goals; such an approach allows them to remain concentrated and avoid sacrificing quality or productivity. Gen X is aware of how technology can escalate potential gains while lessening danger through increased automation functionalities; however, at times when remote working arrangements or other forms of external factors take place outside one's control, they understand limitations when trying to establish meaningful interrelationships with team members who might feel alienated from one another due to said arrangements.

Technological Fluency and Innovation

To succeed in today's world, leaders must keep up with technology and have insight into computers, programming languages, hardware specifications, and digital communication mediums such as social media platforms. The capacity to promptly learn fresh technological procedures can aid Gen X leaders in maintaining their competitive edge within an ever-changing global digital economy.

It is now more essential than ever for Gen Xers to remain relevant in the workplace, and innovation has become a key factor. Technology, which evolves almost daily, requires leaders to stay aware of changes and discover ways to use them productively at work. Gen X leaders need to constantly keep up with modern trends, such as AI or augmented reality, and investigate new technologies that could completely change business processes or product ranges.

Additionally, Gen X professionals must have a team comprised of knowledgeable people who assist them in capitalizing on developments within technology when they are not tech-savvy, as having this kind of expertise available gives Gen Xers significant benefits over competitors who lack access to such resources. Such a team would allow them to maintain their positions ahead in constantly fluctuating markets by taking advantage of technical advances to achieve success.

Leading Across Generations

With Baby Boomers rapidly progressing toward retirement age, organizations must prepare an appropriate plan for managing this shifting workforce. Leading across generations necessitates familiarity with each group's work techniques, priorities, and communication inclinations.

While Millennials possess a collaborative approach to problem-solving that encourages discourse between generations, Gen Xers tend to favor autonomy and keeping their distance from others in the workplace. As such, organizations must acknowledge these distinctions and construct an environment that allows both cohorts to flourish without interfering with team dynamics or marginalizing any individual.

Companies can integrate mentorship programs into their overall technique to aid them in bridging the gap between generations and assist in opening the lines of communication between various levels of leadership. By joining younger employees with experienced experts who can furnish direction on professional growth while additionally teaching them about corporate culture and expectations within the organization, businesses can help guarantee that all personnel are triumphant regardless of age or experience level. This would also make every member feel that they have a voice in decision-making processes inside the company and access to resources that may be inaccessible otherwise.

Organizations must also contemplate the most effective method for incorporating technology into their operations without causing friction with any generation of employees, all while ensuring productivity for everyone involved. Incorporating online tools such as project management software could benefit all age groups rather than favoring one over another. However, if incorrectly implemented, some workers might feel excluded from new initiatives due to a lack of education and training required for proper utilization, which could, in turn, lead to low morale among day-to-day teams working together. Ultimately, companies should strive to implement strategies that enable different generations to interact fluidly with each other to be able to capitalize on the strengths of both sides and bolster collaboration, innovation, productivity, and, ultimately, success.

In conclusion, organizations must comprehend the ever-evolving nature of Gen X leadership to guarantee the success of Gen Xers in the future. With their unrivaled expertise and experience, Gen X leaders play an integral role in reshaping the workforce trends of tomorrow while bringing about pertinent modifications within associated establishments. By capitalizing on their skill set, Gen Xers can provide invaluable contributions when navigating through times of uncertainty that may arise.

12

Creating a Multi-Generational Leadership Legacy

Organizations must develop a leadership legacy that spans generations as the workforce becomes more multi-generational. A multi-generational Gen X legacy requires understanding generational dynamics, succession planning, and team-building approaches, as long-term success is obtained by implementing effective strategies and systems.

The Role of Gen X Leadership

Gen X needs to be regularly noticed and remembered in the workforce as they possess a distinct set of abilities that can make them invaluable to organizations. As Gen Xers, born between 1965 and 1980, are entering their peak years of leadership, they may become an essential component within the prosperity experienced by numerous companies. Gen X presents a one-of-a-kind conglomeration of experience coupled with energy, which could be capitalized on to form a multi-generational leadership legacy for future generations.

Gaining insight into the attitudes of Gen X leaders is essential to capitalize on their varied abilities. Typically, Gen Xers are independent thinkers prioritizing autonomy over conformity; they dislike being instructed regarding what or when something must be done. Rather than desiring financial gain and authority, Gen Xers often have a passion for completing tasks efficiently without pursuing promotion within an organization.

Gen Xers bring forth information and proficiency from their past vocations that can be essential to any organization's prosperity if utilized suitably. They may only sometimes comprehend or assent to established corporate structures. Yet, their understanding of various procedures can be priceless for discovering new resolutions and routes ahead for organizations seeking development chances.

Employers of Gen Xers must provide flexible working options, when possible, to accommodate the great importance placed on work-life balance. Companies should also ensure that ample opportunities for training and development with their teams are provided so that employees can feel supported in achieving professional and personal goals. In addition, mentorship programs should be designed for Gen X leaders to give employees access to necessary resources throughout their career journey, such as advice concerning career trajectories or public speaking tips, guidance regarding navigating office politics, etc.

Incorporating these elements into day-to-day operations within an organization can generate an atmosphere where Gen Xers feel appreciated while inspiring future generations through a strong multi-generational leadership legacy founded upon mutual respect among all involved parties.

Shaping a Diverse and Collaborative Workplace

Gen X is renowned for leaving a legacy of leadership that promotes collaboration and diversity. Gen X has acquired an appreciation for connecting with individuals from divergent contexts, internally within their respective organizations and the external community. Through this comprehension, Gen X leaders can shape a work atmosphere wherein cooperation and variety are welcomed, commended, and bolstered. To facilitate such a legacy being put into practice, one may foster genuine relationships between colleagues from various backgrounds.

Gen X leaders should attempt to construct an environment where employees feel comfortable exchanging experiences, opinions, and ideas regardless of age or cultural background. They should motivate open discourse among team members so that all perspectives can be heard and respected. By cultivating these relationships, Gen X leaders can guarantee that workers experience a tangible sense of inclusion in the workplace, which is crucial for any prosperous organization.

Beyond developing significant affiliations between co-workers from different backgrounds, Gen X leaders must prioritize recruiting practices that advance diversity. Gen X leaders should proactively seek candidates with diverse experiences and perspectives who may have yet to be considered previously but could bring unique skill sets to the organization. Implementing such an approach would enable companies to reap benefits ranging from having a more diversified team to accessing new sources of creativity and venturing into different markets, which might result in increased profits.

Hence, it is essential for Gen X leaders to cultivate an atmosphere where:

- collaboration between people of various backgrounds is respected rather than rebuffed.
- everyone feels comfortable presenting their ideas, disregarding age or experience.
- innovation is fostered through commitment toward diversity when hiring at all levels within the company.

The Adaptable Leadership Approach of Gen X

Gen X is a population that has made its presence known in business. Noted for being adaptable and resourceful while taking risks, Gen X is well-acquainted with adjusting their approach to leading teams and navigating corporate environments. Their willingness to modify strategies as needed enables them to develop successful businesses, bolstered by reliable team dynamics based on collaboration, communication, and trustworthiness. As such, the qualities of Gen X prove invaluable for problem-solving within enterprises, both large and small, as they have become hallmarks associated with Gen Xers who manage companies and staff efficiently.

As the current generation of leaders advances in their management positions, they carry specific attributes that have contributed to their success, including adaptability, innovation, determination, and resilience. The mentality of Gen X encourages trial and error and experimentation, resulting in original solutions applicable to any organization's strategic objectives. This type of progressive thinking has enabled various businesses to operate more proficiently while increasing employee satisfaction and customer happiness.

Gen Xers recognize the significance not solely to a company's profit margins but also to its environment when an effective system of multi-generational leadership is in place. By granting younger generations entrance into mentorship opportunities from experienced leaders within their businesses, they can acquire knowledge on how to achieve professional and personal success down any career path, ignoring age or experience level. With these mentorships, Gen Xers may serve as connectors between the different eras by passing on their experiences with those rising behind them so that errors will be avoided without having to go through similar circumstances themselves at some point ahead.

The heritage left by this period will unquestionably be one grounded in efficient adaptation, whether it involves allowing new technologies or furnishing instruction regarding how best to confront difficulties. Gen X's heritage shall carry on instructing future ages invaluable lessons about how best to steer firms onward despite what lies beyond.

Inclusivity as a Cornerstone of Gen X Leadership

Inclusivity, an essential skill that all leaders should endeavor to embrace and cultivate, is a foundational element of Gen X leadership. Gen X figures must recognize the significance of honoring diversity in their working environment. Those seated with power must act by treasuring and including various points of view, cultures, ages, sexes, and other components inherent in someone's identity. This outlook encourages more imaginative occupancy through improved participation from employees who feel appreciated and esteemed due to their input.

Rather than fostering an environment where everyone is assumed to be accommodating to a single criterion or outlook, Gen X pioneers should demonstrate receptiveness toward each other's experiences while being open-minded about notions offered by more youthful partners. This kind of openness will motivate members regardless of age or place in their career trajectory and show actual command characteristics that can be disseminated through successive generations as they ascend the ranks.

Gen Xers must keep in mind that there exists the possibility for expansion inside any organization as they strive toward incorporating diversity into the workplace. Gen Xers should set aside their preconceptions about those who are distinct from them and instead pay attention with open ears to become successful inclusive leaders. They must move away from generic thinking models based on stringent regulations and hierarchies; instead, Gen Xers should observe how new technologies can bring together multiple generations, featuring meaningful debates that culminate in progressive solutions within the company walls and beyond them.

Encouraging Leaders to Adopt Gen X's Approach

Gen X leaders are renowned for having several distinctive characteristics that bring inestimable value to the working environment. They typically demonstrate an exceptional amalgamation of technical proficiency and interpersonal abilities with a capacity for out-of-the-box thinking when necessary. Above all, however, Gen Xers carry themselves with unwavering dedication toward their team and organization.

The qualities possessed by Gen Xers can be of tremendous value in today's highly competitive business ecosystem; however, many entities need to recognize this capacity when it comes to generating competent leaders of the future. Rather than concentrating on how an approach derived from those born between 1965 and 1980 could prove advantageous for employees and strategies employed by current organizations, some companies need to recognize the significance of building a setting where these attributes may be supported and honed with time. The answer lies in stimulating all generations within a specific organization—from Millennials to Baby Boomers—and adopting a cross-generational perspective incorporating knowledge provided by each age group.

It is paramount for companies that have already adopted the multi-generational leadership model, as well as those considering doing so in the future, to understand that it is essential for each generation's unique capabilities and skills to be equally respected within their organization regardless of age or experience level. By doing so, a healthier work environment can be created at all levels while providing opportunities for growth among every generational group inside its walls. Gen Xers pioneered this collaborative approach but now require contributions from members across other generations to make a lasting impression on developing influential leaders throughout organizations.

At its soul, this collaborative system promotes interaction between different ages through mentorship programs, thus giving access to newer ideas brought by younger minds and likewise granting seasoned professionals with wisdom gained over time;

furthermore, it allows mistakes without fear thanks to acquired knowledge coupled with support amongst various generational groups dealing professionally with varying life stages.

Building a Multi-Generational Leadership Legacy

Formulating such values requires a deep understanding of the current generation's beliefs and norms and an awareness of generational differences in perspectives. Once these core principles have been identified, it is essential to communicate them clearly across all organizational levels so that everyone understands how they should be applied while allowing flexibility and creativity when needed.

Constructing a multi-generational Gen X leadership legacy involves significant effort yet yields tremendous rewards such as long-term stability, continuity between generations, and increased innovation due to diversity in skillsets and ideas. To achieve this feat successfully, however, organizations must identify the fundamental values necessary for its longevity and communicate them effectively throughout various organizational layers so that employees comprehend their application while simultaneously enabling freedom for individual interpretation where necessary.

Ultimately, establishing this legacy helps enhance sustainability through changes in the economy or industry trends by providing continual support from one era into another, with efficacy firmly at its center point. Leaders must appreciate their distinctions from other generations and how they can apply those values to fashion something everlasting. To illustrate, Gen Xers are commonly viewed as independent intellectuals who prioritize taking risks and cooperation over rigid hierarchies; by incorporating these qualities into their leadership style, Gen Xers may generate a milieu that stimulates inventiveness and open conversations among all personnel. To ensure this heritage continues through subsequent generations, leaders must offer mentoring prospects for junior inheritors. Experienced executives must provide younger colleagues with coaching sessions or resources to share their knowledge and help them understand the qualities that have led to successful roles.

Although establishing a multi-generational leadership legacy may initially appear intimidating, there are numerous contemporary tools available to make this goal more accessible, from online courses developed exclusively for soon-to-be managers to comprehensive mentoring programs tailored according to age groups or industries.

Passing Down Leadership Values to Future Generations

The leadership values of Gen X must be passed down to future generations for a multi-generational legacy. It is essential to guarantee that successive generations maintain and adhere to the standards that Gen X leaders have set forth. One way this can be achieved is through mentorship programs and other methods that promote knowledge transmission from one era to another. Mentorship programs offer an example whereby senior Gen Xers may share valuable lessons from their successes, failings, and accomplishments with younger members.

Mentorships should not merely consist of offering advice but also involve meaningful and honest conversations about the challenges that were encountered and how those issues were successfully addressed to better prepare younger individuals to grapple with career tribulations. Another effective route for passing on leadership values would be through sharing past experiences—by narrating stories concerning successes and errors made by previous leaders—as these may serve as valuable lessons upon which subsequent generations might draw insights.

Moreover, it is essential to foster an environment in which youth can display self-confidence, allowing them to take risks without feeling anxious or experiencing judgmental criticism for potential missteps. Future leaders should understand that no one succeeds without making mistakes, as they constitute the best way of finding out what works better for any given situation or leadership model. As such, storytelling allows Gen Xers to reminisce about their personal experiences while inspiring others by narrating tales from their journey into leadership roles within organizations and vast communities.

Leadership values are further perpetuated through educational initiatives such as workshops held periodically at academic institutions or even within organizations themselves, in which those aspiring to become influential leaders can learn more about how successful people have achieved their current level of professional and personal satisfaction. Talks or seminars should be conducted by experienced professionals who offer advice on specific aspects of successfully leading others through team-building exercises to communication strategies when coping with difficult circumstances. Such education initiatives provide invaluable insight into effective leadership styles while aiding younger generations to continue developing the skills needed for success in today's increasingly competitive world.

Gen X's Unique Position Between Baby Boomers and Millennials

To leave a lasting leadership legacy, Gen Xers must confront unique difficulties; they comprise far fewer individuals than their predecessors or successors yet possess equally pertinent qualities. Gen X is often labeled "the forgotten middle" due to its lack of political influence compared to other generations.

Despite this apparent disadvantage, Gen Xers possess various traits that make them incredibly valuable to any organization. These individuals have established a compelling blend of traditional values, such as hard work and respect for authority, with modern sensibilities like embracing technology and diversity. This unique combination is especially advantageous in organizations where both perspectives must be considered. While younger Gen Xers may bring more skill in using up-to-date technologies, older Gen Xers are essential since they contribute experience and knowledge to significant decisions.

Gen Xers have a reputation for being independent and self-motivated, which makes them well-suited for leadership roles that require the ownership of projects or processes without excessive management supervision. They are also highly adaptable and can keep their team focused amid dramatic changes with remarkable poise. In addition, Gen X does an excellent job in balancing creativity when solving problems while still adhering strictly to organizational protocols, thereby allowing new ideas to be implemented quickly during times when efficient thinking is essential. Yet, long-term objectives remain intact thanks to Gen X leaders' sound judgment. This combination of attributes makes Gen Xers vital in any organization desiring multi-generational success stories regardless of project scope.

Creating a Culture of Continuous Leadership Development

The development of a culture that emphasizes continuous learning and growth is essential for any organization looking to create a multi-generational legacy of Gen X leadership. Investing in current leaders and those being groomed for future executive roles allows organizations to guarantee their success in the years ahead. Given that each generation has different approaches and anticipations concerning leading, establishing an environment beneficial to the leadership style advocated by Gen Xers holds great significance.

Comprehending the wants and inspirations of Gen X when building up this environment is essential. Given that Gen Xers were raised in an era of swift changes, they are at ease with ambiguity and instability. Additionally, they esteem flexibility, independence, and collaboration rather than stiff hierarchies or traditional supervision styles.

It should be recognized that present-day organizations value a less hierarchical approach, in which everyone's opinion is regarded as necessary, and teams can work together on resolving issues without encountering protracted authorization processes or governmental bureaucracy. Consequently, leadership growth initiatives should maximize this kind of teamwork whenever possible by allowing people at every level within the organization to give their thoughts, provide commentary, and participate in decision-making activities.

Organizations should provide their employees with the opportunity to voice their opinions and concerns directly to facilitate better decisions by future organization leaders. Also, steps must be taken to identify promising potential leaders early on among current staff to allow more time to build up their skills through mentoring connections with more seasoned personnel or participation in specialized training programs designed for emerging professionals within a particular industry sector or company culture. Furthermore, allowing younger generations ownership over specific tasks helps stimulate job satisfaction, increasing retention rates over an extended period, and ensuring continuity between teams and across departments while mitigating any knowledge gaps that may arise unexpectedly due to fluctuating market conditions.

Finally, careful planning for multi-generational leadership is essential to ensure lasting success for an organization. A comprehensive understanding of generational dynamics and an unwavering commitment to team building are required. Moreover, succession planning is pivotal in constructing such a long-lasting leadership heritage, as with proper strategy implementation, Gen X can leave behind a powerful and enduring multi-generational leadership legacy.

Bibliography

- Cashman, Kevin. 2017. *Leadership from the Inside Out: Becoming a Leader for Life*. National Geographic Books.

- Christensen, Clayton M. 2015. *The Innovator's Dilemma: When New Technologies Cause Great Firms to Fail*. Harvard Business Review Press.

- Dungy, Tony. 2011. *The Mentor Leader: Secrets to Building People and Teams That Win Consistently*. Tyndale Momentum.

- Gordinier, Jeff. 2009. *X Saves the World: How Generation X Got the Shaft but Can Still Keep Everything from Sucking*. National Geographic Books.

- Howe, Neil, and William Strauss. 1997. *The Fourth Turning: An American Prophecy*. Broadway Books.

- Kerr, James. 2013. *Legacy: What the All Blacks Can Teach Us About the Business of Life*. Constable.

- Kouzes, James M., and Barry Z. Posner. 2017. *The Leadership Challenge: How to Make Extraordinary Things Happen in Organizations*. John Wiley & Sons.

- Sinek, Simon. 2014. *Leaders Eat Last: Why Some Teams Pull Together and Others Don't*. Portfolio.

- Strauss, William, and Neil Howe. 1991. *Generations: The History of America's Future, 1584 to 2069*. William Morrow.

- Turkle, Sherry. 2015. *Reclaiming Conversation: The Power of Talk in a Digital Age.* Penguin.

- Zemke, Ron, Claire Raines, and Bob Filipczak. 2000. "Generations at Work: Managing the Clash of Veterans, Boomers, Xers, and Nexters in Your Workplace." *Choice Reviews Online* 37 (08): 37–4592. https://doi.org/10.5860/choice.37-4592.

Printed in the United States
by Baker & Taylor Publisher Services